OUR LIVING WORLD OF NATURE

The
Life
of the
Desert

Developed jointly with The World Book Encyclopedia

*Produced with the cooperation of
The United States Department of the Interior*

OUR LIVING WORLD OF NATURE

The
Life
of the
Desert

ANN *and* MYRON SUTTON

Published in cooperation with
The World Book Encyclopedia

McGraw-Hill Book Company
NEW YORK   TORONTO   LONDON

ANN *and* **MYRON SUTTON** *met when each was a park naturalist at Grand Canyon National Park, Arizona. This husband-and-wife team has studied natural history firsthand in nearly every corner of the world. Ann, a geologist, has served as Curator of Geology at the Illinois State Museum, Instructor in Paleontology at the University of Kentucky, and Research Specialist for the United States Geological Survey. Myron was graduated from Northern Arizona University, where he studied biology. A native of Arizona, he has traveled extensively in the deserts of the American Southwest. In eighteen years with the National Park Service of the United States Department of the Interior, Washington, D.C., Myron has served as ranger, naturalist, instructor, and planner. In his present position as a specialist in natural science, national parks, and conservation on a world-wide scale, he has been frequently called upon to lecture and advise in Europe, the Orient, the South Pacific, and Central America, as well as throughout the United States. The Suttons have collaborated on scores of technical and popular articles, booklets, and book reviews and have written nine books, including* Nature on the Rampage *(J. B. Lippincott, 1962)*, Exploring with the Bartrams *(Rand McNally, 1963)*, Guarding the Treasured Lands: Story of the National Park Service *(J. B. Lippincott, 1965)*, and Journey into Ice *(Rand McNally, 1965)*.

Library of Congress Catalog Card Number: 66–17516

1234567890 NR 721069876

46002

Contents

THE FACE OF THE DESERT 151

APPENDIX

A Day in the Desert

SILENCE. Not a sound, not a breath of life—or so it seems. Strange shapes rise before you, statues reaching toward the sky. On the hillside, rocks shimmer with heat. The glare of light is so intense that you blink your eyes. You are in the desert.

It is midday in summer. Overhead the sun burns fiercely. Step into the shade, the thin shadow of a giant saguaro cactus. The heat lessens somewhat, and the glare diminishes.

As far as the eye can see—perhaps a hundred miles in this unclouded atmosphere—there is not a sand dune. In fact, here in the Arizona desert (a good place to begin your acquaintance with life of the desert), you will see few totally barren patches. True, in some desert areas of the world there is nothing but drifting sand or barren ground. This is the case in portions of the Sahara in North Africa and of the Gobi Desert in Asia; it is also true of the great salt deserts in Utah. But in most North American deserts plant and animal life is relatively abundant, although you may not see it at first if your eyes have been trained in forests or the vast grasslands of the Midwest.

But look closely. The giant saguaro cactus you are standing next to is certainly a strange plant, with its upraised
limbs and thousands of needles, and so are the other cactuses
that grow along the rocky hillside. Below, where the ground
levels off, you can see scattered cholla, paloverde, ocotillo—
plants with melodious Spanish names. Mesquite spreads in
all directions. It is bushy, tough, and deep-rooted.

Even though there are many kinds of plants in the desert,
the vegetation *is* sparse, compared with the heavy growth
of a forest. Most of the large plants stand apart from one
another, as if each were engaged in a solitary struggle for
survival. One reason for this wide spacing is that there is
simply not enough water in the desert to support great
numbers of plants growing close together. In an area of
plentiful rainfall—Louisiana or Puerto Rico, for instance—
vegetation is thick and lush because plants do not have to

10

Wiry clumps of ocotillo dot
the desert at Big Bend National
Park, Texas. Each plant saps
all the moisture in its arid patch
of soil. Ocotillo, creosote bush,
and many other desert plants
are so regularly spaced that they
almost seem to be planted
that way by man.

compete for water. They may grow close together, their roots actually entwining, yet there is plenty of water for all.

In the desert, however, it is a matter of first come, first served. Many seeds are carried by animals or wind to a particular spot, but the first plant to establish a root network usually absorbs most of the moisture in the soil, leaving very little for other plants. There is hardly a trace of humidity—not a cloud in the sky. If it rained last month, or last year, most of the water probably evaporated before it could seep into the ground.

Dryness and *heat* are the conditions of life in the desert. How can anything survive? Living things must be specially equipped to survive in this forbidding environment. And the plants do appear extremely hardy. But can animals live in such a world? There is no movement, except the "wavering" of distant mountains in the blur of heat.

11

Animals in the desert

Suddenly rapid shrieks burst out one after another. At first you see nothing—only the dry bed of an old stream that looks as if it has not carried water for years. The shrieks sound again, rapid and shrill, and this time you pinpoint their direction. They are coming from the direction of the trees by the dried-up stream bed—a grove of willows and one or two large cottonwoods.

By using binoculars you can "creep up" on wild creatures without budging from the shade of your giant cactus. Focus on the willows.

There it goes! A Gila woodpecker, red on top, with black-and-white striped wings. It flies with a swooping motion, shrieking all the time; you must be quick to "hold" it in your binoculars. It crosses a sandy wash and comes to rest on a saguaro, where it begins gouging a hole in the stem, looking for insect larvae. The cactus has several such holes in it, and neighboring saguaros have dozens more—mostly the work of Gila woodpeckers. You may see the head of a purple martin or an elf owl poking from one of them, for these birds like to use abandoned woodpecker holes as homes.

In gouging holes in the cactus, the Gila woodpecker is doing more than merely filling its stomach or making a place for a nest. Many of the big cactuses, such as saguaros, cholla, and organ-pipes, are attacked by insects, especially beetle

With staccato taps, a Gila woodpecker gouges out a nesting hole in the side of a saguaro cactus. These giant cactuses frequently are riddled with large and small cavities where woodpeckers either nested or dug out tunneling insects.

The hard, gourdlike nest of a Gila woodpecker is exposed when the softer surrounding tissues of a dying saguaro rot away. Sap forms a hardened inner shell that prevents the loss of water from the injured plant. The nest is so durable that it remains intact long after the saguaro has rotted away.

DESERTS OF THE WORLD

The world's largest deserts are situated where the average annual rainfall is scarce. Most of them lie in two great belts near the Tropic of Cancer in the north and the Tropic of Capricorn in the south (*bottom right*). Desert temperatures are usually thought of as being extremely high, but this is not always the case. The Arctic, for example, has large barren stretches that are desert. The Great Basin Desert does not have the extreme temperatures of the Sonoran Desert, the Sahara, or the Gobi. What all the deserts do have in common is a lack of available water for plant growth. Ten inches of annual rainfall, if distributed evenly over the year with good rains every month or so, is enough to support a lush grassland. In an area where ten inches of rain falls all in one or two months, desert conditions may exist, because plants can use only a certain amount of rain at a time. Rain that falls in torrents only a few months a year usually runs off or sinks into the ground before it can be used by plants. In deserts where temperatures are high, rain often evaporates before it reaches the ground.

In the desertland of North America the great mountain chains of the West Coast act as barriers to ocean air that might otherwise bring some rainfall inland. The diagram (*right*) shows what is called the "rain shadow" effect. As ocean air rises up mountain slopes, its moisture condenses and then rain falls on the ocean-facing side. Little moisture is left by the time the air crosses the mountain peaks, and so the rainfall behind each mountain chain is greatly reduced. Much of the moisture in ocean air, even before it reaches land, has been removed by the drying effects of cold currents, such as the California Current in the Pacific Ocean (*bottom left*).

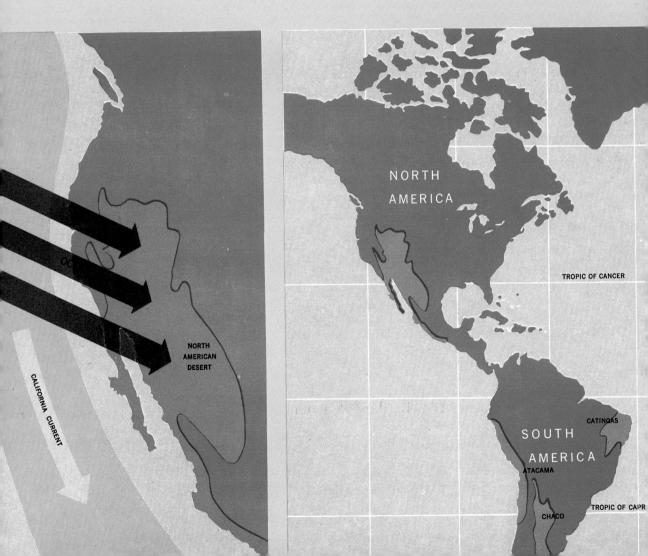

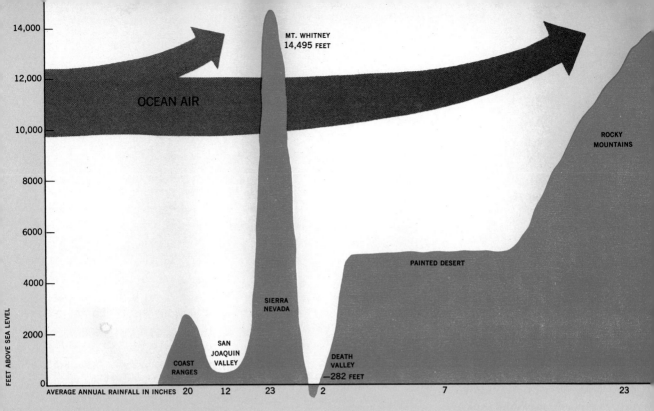

FEET ABOVE SEA LEVEL

14,000
12,000
10,000
8000
6000
4000
2000
0

OCEAN AIR

MT. WHITNEY
14,495 FEET

ROCKY
MOUNTAINS

SIERRA
NEVADA

PAINTED DESERT

COAST
RANGES

SAN
JOAQUIN
VALLEY

DEATH
VALLEY
—282 FEET

AVERAGE ANNUAL RAINFALL IN INCHES   20   12   23   2   7   23

ASIA

EUROPE

TURKESTAN

GOBI

INDIAN

SAHARA

ARABIAN

AFRICA

NAMIB

KALAHARI

AUSTRALIAN

larvae. These larvae not only cause injury to the cactuses by eating their inner tissues, but some are also probably the carriers of diseases that have killed cactuses in many areas. Consequently the woodpecker, with its voracious appetite, may be saving cactuses from destruction. At the same time it is providing homes for many birds other than purple martins and elf owls. The holes in the saguaro soon become lined with hardened sap that forms a tough inner shell somewhat resembling the inside of a gourd. These holes then make excellent nesting cavities for sparrow hawks, gilded flickers, screech owls, Wied's crested flycatchers, and other hole-nesting species. Altogether, this interrelationship among woodpeckers, cactuses, insects, and other birds is a particularly good example of the vital connection that links all living things to each other, in the desert and elsewhere. Each of these species—plant or animal—performs a service for other species simply by satisfying its own needs, and thus this little chain of life is kept intact.

A high-pitched whistle sounds from the hillside, there among the rocks. Suddenly your eye is caught by a moving shape—the head of a rock squirrel jerking up and down, searching the sky above and the land below for hawks, snakes, or other signs of danger. Because its fur is almost the color of the rocks, the squirrel is nearly invisible.

The rock squirrel is active during the day, searching for seeds and other plant food among rocks, shrubs, and small trees. Like some other ground squirrels, it often sleeps away the hottest part of the summer in an underground burrow.

Rock squirrels belong to a large group of animals called ground squirrels, several of which resemble chipmunks. Like other desert ground squirrels and some birds, rock squirrels *estivate*. Estivation, like hibernation, is a time of inactivity. Some animals, such as woodchucks and bats, hibernate during the winter in cold climates; they retire into a secluded place and sink into a deep sleep, during which such bodily functions as heartbeat and breathing become extremely sluggish. Desert animals that estivate do the same thing in summer, and thus sleep away the driest part of the year, without eating or drinking. Estivation and hibernation are only two of the many remarkable ways in which animals have become adapted to extreme conditions.

A butterfly flits along the wash, past a grove of mesquite, and settles on a prickly pear, where there are other butterflies as well. Looking farther, your binoculars pick out smaller insects buzzing around the yellow flowers of the mesquite or swarming upon the huge flower clusters of an

An anise swallowtail sips nectar from the showy blossom of a prickly-pear cactus. The brightly banded caterpillars of this species feed on leaves of anise, fennel, and related plants.

agave, or century plant. On the ground, bees move in and out of their burrows, busy storing food for the new generations that will be born underground.

Quick movements in a cane cactus attract your attention. A female black-throated sparrow, gray-backed with handsome black markings, flies to her nest among the cactus spines, carrying insects to her young.

Even in the intense heat of the desert at noon on a summer day, there are many animals—more than you, if you are unfamiliar with the Arizona desert, had thought at first.

The chain of life

The source of the desert's superabundant light and heat is the sun, the ultimate source of nearly all the earth's heat and light; every living thing, animal or plant, depends on it. But animals, including man, cannot use the sun's energy directly, except possibly in the formation of vitamin D_3 in the skin when the body is exposed to sunlight. The work of converting solar energy to a form which can be used by animals is done by the plants.

All green plants—the tallest tree and the smallest one-celled diatom in the ocean—can capture energy from sunlight and use it in manufacturing molecules of glucose. This simple plant sugar is one of the substances known as carbohydrates. The process of making glucose is called *photosynthesis*, which means literally "putting together with light." It is carried on by means of the plants' green pigments, the chlorophylls, which use carbon dioxide from the air, water from the soil, and the energy of sunlight.

The resulting sugar, called glucose, serves as a basic food that is used to manufacture all the fats, proteins, and other carbohydrates necessary for plant growth and reproduction. All these plant products, in effect, contain a little of the sun's energy. It is this energy on which all life is dependent. Stored in the tissues of green plants, the sun's energy is made available in the form of food to the plant-eating animals

A male Bullock's oriole fills its stomach with the small insects that swarm over the flower clusters of the century plant. Contrary to the popular story that they bloom only once in a hundred years, these plants may flower in ten to thirty years or not at all.

All green plants manufacture food in the form of sugar by using water and carbon dioxide in the process called photosynthesis. The energy of sunlight powers chlorophyll, which splits the water into hydrogen and oxygen. The oxygen from the water is returned to the atmosphere, and part of the hydrogen reunites with the oxygen from the carbon dioxide to form additional water. The remaining hydrogen is combined with the carbon and oxygen from the carbon dioxide, forming sugar. All of this split-second process takes place in tiny green bodies, called chloroplasts, within the plant cells.

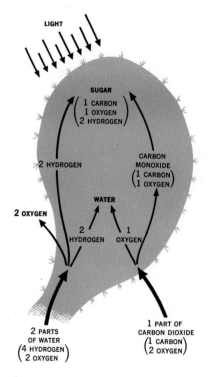

LIGHT

SUGAR
(1 CARBON
1 OXYGEN
2 HYDROGEN)

2 HYDROGEN

CARBON MONOXIDE
(1 CARBON
1 OXYGEN)

WATER

2 OXYGEN

2 HYDROGEN   1 OXYGEN

2 PARTS OF WATER
(4 HYDROGEN
2 OXYGEN)

1 PART OF CARBON DIOXIDE
(1 CARBON
2 OXYGEN)

that feed on seeds, stems, leaves, and so on (as when the beetle larva eats the saguaro) or to the meat-eating animals that feed on the plant-eaters (as when the Gila woodpecker eats the beetle larva). The phrase *chain of life* aptly describes this basic dependence of animals upon plants. Energy-rich foods are first made by plants and then passed on to the next link, plant-eating animals. These are eaten by flesh-eating animals, which in turn may be eaten by larger flesh-eating animals—the woodpecker may be caught by a hawk. But as the original energy of the sun passes along the chain from plant to animal to animal (and then eventually, when an animal dies, passes to bacteria and other microorganisms), it is continually diminished. In the end this energy is lost—mostly dispersed into the air as heat. Thus the living world depends on plants to continue manufacturing new supplies of carbohydrates, proteins, and fats to replace the energy lost along the chain of life.

Sometimes the chain of life may break completely; a link may snap and the transfer of energy from one species to another may be interrupted. (When this happens to the human species, we call it famine.)

How hot is the desert?

Careful measurements of desert temperatures have shown that the air five feet aboveground may be 125° Fahrenheit, one foot aboveground 150°, one inch aboveground 165°, and on the surface 180°! All these temperatures were recorded in the shade. Consequently animals that live on or near the surface must be able to withstand extreme heat.

No wonder, then, that desert animals seek shade. A pair of Gambel's quail nests in a prickly pear's shadow. A coyote, its fur blending with the shadow, sits in the shade of a mesquite. Obviously the coyote does not work for its living at this time of day. Who would go hunting at noon under the desert sun wearing a fur coat?

Fur-bearing animals in the forest do not face this prob-

In deserts, the sun shines directly on the exposed soil and rock, its intensity hardly diminished by the dry air and the sparse vegetation. In forests, however, much sunlight is absorbed by clouds and haze before it can reach the treetops, and even more is absorbed by the leaves and branches of trees before it can reach the ground. Thus the intensity of sunlight falling directly on forest floors is a small fraction of that of sunlight falling on desert surfaces.

DESERT

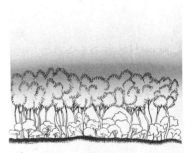

FOREST

The meat-eating coyote gets its energy by feeding on plant-eating animals such as this black-tailed jack rabbit. In this way the energy of the sun is passed from green plants, which convert solar energy into a usable form, to the plant-eating animals and, in turn, to the meat-eaters.

DESERT

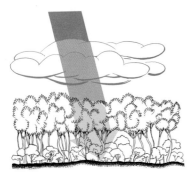

FOREST

lem. The sun may shine as brightly on a forest as it does on a desert, but daytime temperatures in a forest are lower than in a desert. One reason for this is that trees shield the forest floor from the sun's rays. Indeed, less than 1 per cent of the sunlight falling on a dense forest may actually reach the ground. In the desert, however, there is relatively little vegetation to shield the soil. Aside from the small amount used by green plants, about half the sun's energy bounces back, and the other half is absorbed and concentrated, mostly in the first few inches of soil and in the air close to the ground. When you are walking in the desert, the heat comes up from the ground as well as from above, just as it does when you are walking on city pavement in July.

Another reason for the desert's heat is its lack of water. The air is dry, the ground is dry. There is generally very little moisture in the air in the form of haze or clouds to interfere with the direct flow of the sun's rays to the earth, and there is seldom much moisture in the hard-packed soil to evaporate and help carry off the heat.

The forest is quite different in this respect. There the trees themselves contain a great deal of water. The forest floor is blanketed with damp leaves, twigs, and rotting logs, and the spongy soil is often nearly saturated with water. Wherever sunlight strikes the forest, its heat is partially absorbed by water and then carried off in vapor as the water evaporates. On a sunny day, for example, one medium-sized maple tree will *transpire*, or give off, fifty gallons of water vapor and get rid of a tremendous amount of heat, just as you get rid of heat by the evaporation of perspiration.

The highest air temperature recorded officially five feet aboveground in the United States was 134° in the shade. That was in Death Valley, California. The valley drops to 282 feet below sea level, the lowest point in the Western Hemisphere.

Few places on earth are more aptly named than Death Valley. The number of men who have died there is unknown. Even so, the name is not quite accurate, for life does exist in Death Valley. A dozen species of lizards, more than

A black-tailed jack rabbit and a ground squirrel share the meager shadow cast by a cactus. Since mid-afternoon temperatures on the desert floor may soar as high as 180°, most daytime animals are active only in the early morning and late afternoon. At midday they seek a sheltered spot and wait out the heat.

thirty species of mammals, more than 600 species of plants, and even—strange as it seems—fish thrive there. And from mid-October to mid-April the climate of Death Valley is quite delightful.

The extreme conditions in Death Valley during most of the year make it a fascinating desert for both scientists and tourists. Fortunately, in 1933 a large part—3000 square miles—was set aside to form Death Valley National Monument, one of the largest parks in the United States. Today it has excellent roads and scenic trails, a fine museum, a hotel, campgrounds, and other facilities. It is well worth a visit.

For a long time Death Valley's 134° was the record high air temperature for the world, but in 1922 this distinction was yielded to Azizia in North Africa, where 136° in the shade was recorded. Elsewhere extremes as high as 170° have been reported but have not been officially confirmed.

Such are the records of the desert. They bear out the observation that the highest temperatures occur in dry regions. Even in equatorial jungles daytime temperatures seldom rise above 100°. There, as in temperate forests, much of the sun's energy goes not into heating the air and soil but into evaporating water. Thus people living near the jungle often burn electric lights in their closets to dry the air and prevent the growth of mildew. In the desert no such precautions are necessary; the dry air has remarkable preserva-

tive qualities. Objects taken from the excavated dwellings of prehistoric desert Indians are often perfectly preserved after more than a thousand years.

Desert heat kills

The best refuge from the desert heat is underground, where the heat does not penetrate. Most small animals spend the hot part of the day in burrows or crevices below the sun-baked surface. Animals that do not go underground seek whatever shade they can find, although most desert plants are too thin or sparsely leafed to cast good shadows, especially at noon.

The coyote often cannot find or dig a burrow big enough to accommodate it, and must sit and endure the heat. But, like other members of the dog family, the coyote has one advantage over some other creatures: it can pant. As it pants, air moving in and out of its lungs evaporates moisture on its tongue and in its mouth and throat and thus helps lower the coyote's body temperature. Some other animals, including cattle, horses, and men, give off moisture by sweating; the resulting evaporation similarly reduces their body temperatures.

Reptiles do not regulate their body temperatures as

Even though Death Valley National Monument, California, is one of the hottest deserts in the world, only a small portion is covered with dunes such as these. Most of the monument's 300 square miles support a large variety of desert plants: more than 600 species are known to thrive there.

Shaded by a desert shrub, a bobcat patiently endures the midday heat. At sunset it will emerge and spend the night stalking cottontails, jack rabbits, squirrels, and other prey. The powerful cat may roam as far as twenty miles in a single night of hunting.

coyotes and other mammals do. Generally speaking, they have no sweat glands and they do not pant, and as a result they are at the mercy of their environment. If the environment is hot, they are hot and their body temperatures go up. Within limits this is no problem, for reptiles do not have a precise "normal" temperature, as human beings do. But if their temperatures rise too high they die.

Louis Schellbach, a naturalist formerly on the staff of Grand Canyon National Park, once came upon a rattlesnake. "Desiring a picture," he wrote later, "I hooked him out from the dense growth into the bright sunshine for photographing. It was a very hot July day, about midafternoon; in a short time he turned belly-up, and died before I could pose him and focus the camera."

Other scientists have experimented with rattlesnakes by carrying them from shade into the open sunlight of the desert. The snakes tried to get back, but if they could not find the shade immediately, they began to writhe in one spot, unable to crawl away. In five minutes the writhing had stopped. In seven minutes all bodily movement had ended, and in ten minutes the rattlesnakes were dead.

Left alone, however, reptiles can avoid the midday heat. They simply retire underground, or into the shade, before the sun gets too hot for them; they stay there until the heat diminishes again. Rattlesnakes, horned lizards, Gila monsters, geckoes, tortoises all join the midday search for comfort. So long as they can enjoy their siestas undisturbed, they are safe from the sun's killing rays.

Lizards and other reptiles with legs have an easier time in the desert heat. If necessary they can run across open spaces without touching the sun-baked earth with their bodies. Often you will see a lizard scurrying as fast as it can, its tail lifted high in the air. Some even run on their hind legs so that their forefeet need not touch the ground. Many desert insects such as ants also run with remarkable speed, their bodies raised as high above the earth as their legs will permit. During the hottest part of the day, insects and all desert creatures do anything possible to reduce contact between their bodies and the hot ground surface.

Of all desert dwellers the birds are the ones that escape the extreme heat most easily, and as a consequence they remain most active during the heat of the day. Because they

A red-tailed hawk soars above its ragged nest in the branch of a saguaro. Most desert birds remain active even during the hottest part of the day.

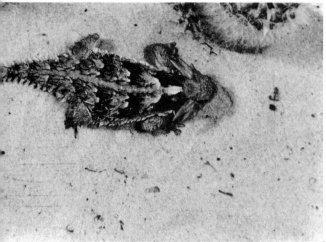

**Wriggling its flattened body
from side to side, a horned lizard
disappears headfirst into a cool,
insulating blanket of sand. . . .**

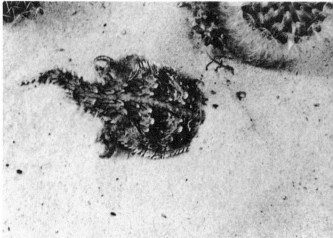

can fly, birds rise easily above the hot surface of the ground
and perch in high places. When they are airborne, the stream
of air across their bodies helps cool them, and their feathers
are excellent insulation from the direct heat of the sun. In
addition, since most birds have body temperatures between
104° and 108°, they rarely have to withstand temperatures
greater than that of their bodies for more than about three
and a half hours a day. All these factors make birds as a
group better able to cope with heat and dryness.

Hotter and hotter

Now the sun crosses the zenith and begins its descent in the
western sky. Noon is past. But this does not mean a let-up in
the heat: the hottest part of the day is midafternoon. By

two-thirty or three o'clock the heat is so intense that the remote mountains seem to dance in the blue air, and if conditions are right, you may see a "lake" in the distance, a vision of cool blue water. Many an old-time prospector saw one and learned to know that it was a *mirage*—a layer of heated air mirroring the blue sky.

Very little stirs now, either aboveground or below. The ant hill is quiet. Possibly a few harvester ants may still be seen, or a few leafcutter ants dragging leaves to be chewed up as fertilizer for their underground fungus beds. In the willow grove along the dry creek bed cicadas sound their high, whirring notes, like a thousand rattlesnakes. Now and then the Gila woodpecker shrieks among the willows, or the rock squirrel whistles at an imaginary danger.

The change to sunset

Afternoon wanes. There is a subtle change, a feeling of tension and expectancy hard to define. The light and heat have barely diminished.

Big beetles called *Eleodes*, businesslike in their movements, come out of their burrows and stride along a sandy wash. Known locally as pinacate bugs, they are jet-black, easy to recognize. When one of them is disturbed, it stops short and stands on its head, which seems hardly an effec-

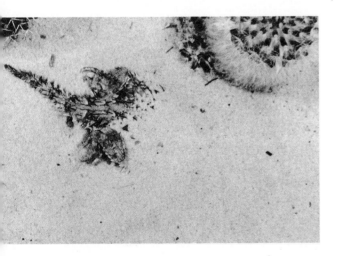

. . . Though the lizard is buried
up to the tip of its tail, its
comfort will be short-lived.
When desert temperatures soar,
it will explode from cover
and head for shade.

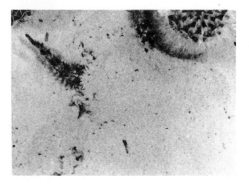

The most common mirage is the reflection of the sky on a highway, appearing to the viewer as a "wet" spot. This type of mirage occurs when the air just above the highway becomes superheated and thins out. Above this heated air layer, a denser layer of air bends the light rays. By far a more spectacular mirage is the inverted image shown here. The real tabletop mountains, or mesas, appear at the bottom, while the mirage, a mirror image, is upside down and just touching the top of them. The phenomenon works on much the same principle as the inverted image viewed through some types of camera lenses.

An object gives off light rays in many different directions. Under normal circumstances only one set of these light rays can be seen by an observer. However, in the desert, the layer of air nearest the desert surface is often hotter and, therefore, less dense than those above it. When two or three of these sudden changes in air density occur one above the other, light rays that previously seemed headed for outer space may be refracted back to the observer. In this case the observer sees two images: the actual object and the mirage, which appears inverted because of the angles at which the light is bent by the atmosphere.

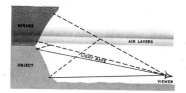

A road runner, or ground cuckoo, pauses for a drink at a desert water hole. More often these sixteen-inch-long birds are seen running rapidly about in search of food. They maneuver so expertly on the ground that even dogs are unable to catch them.

tive defense. But *Eleodes* also ejects a strong secretion that would-be attackers soon learn to avoid.

There goes a road runner after a lizard! Across the rocks, toward the mesquite. All is over in a flash—discovery, chase, capture. The road runner stands jauntily, the lizard's tail and legs dangling from its beak. And there goes a lizard after a—! But the insect is captured and swallowed before you can see what it was. So the business of life goes on as the sun declines in the west. At last the temperature falls below 100°.

Velvet ants, adult females of mutillid wasps, run to and fro on the hard-packed earth. Some are an inch long. Covered with a dense furlike hair, brilliantly colored, some are white, some black and scarlet. In spite of being so conspicuous, however, they have little to worry about from their enemies, for they pack the worst sting, considering their size, of any member of the wasp family. Scurrying here and there, the females are looking for the nests of wasps or bees in which to lay their eggs. Thus the young velvet ant grows up in another insect's nest and eats the eggs or larvae, as well as the food stored there—another example of the desert's interdependencies.

Even swifter in their movements than the ants are the vinegaroons, or whip-tailed scorpions. These are not true scorpions and have no poisonous sting, but they are equipped with strong jaws and pincers. Like the pinacate bugs they secrete a substance that drives away enemies. During the hot part of the day they hide beneath rocks. In appearance and habits the true scorpions of the desert are similar to the vinegaroons, but they are equipped with a poisonous sting at the tip of their long, curving tails. Some of the large species reach four inches in length; but the large species are less poisonous to man than the small varieties, one of which possesses a lethal sting.

You may consider the tarantula, feared by many people, one of the most dangerous desert creatures, yet experi-

With a firm clamp on the flattened head of a lizard, a road runner returns to its nest. Road runners swallow much of their food whole. Their diet consists of insects, toads, lizards, and sometimes rattlesnakes, which they kill with stabbing blows of their sturdy two-inch bills.

A tarantula hawk inserts its venomous stinger in a nerve center on the underside of a tarantula's body. The victorious wasp drags its victim—paralyzed but still alive—into a tunnel in the soil, then deposits an egg on its body. When the egg hatches, the hungry wasp larva feeds on the hairy spider.

menters who work with spiders say that many tarantulas are gentle and make good pets. In addition to their somewhat poisonous bite, tarantulas have the protection of a hairy covering that is prickly and irritating to the touch; but even this is not enough to save them from their enemy the *Pepsis*, or tarantula hawk (which is not a hawk at all, but a wasp). You can recognize *Pepsis* easily: a large insect with orange wings and a blue body. Often it can be seen capturing and stinging a tarantula, then dragging the huge spider off to its nest, where an egg will be laid on the tarantula's body. The tarantula is only paralyzed, and it remains alive until the *Pepsis* egg hatches and the wasp larva emerges. Then the young wasp, whose mother has gone about her business, has fresh food right at hand.

The hours pass. The sun sets beyond the mountains, and the tempo of life quickens. Quail move out from their cover in the mesquite, heading toward water, perhaps to a spring among the sycamores. On their way they chatter like barnyard fowl and peck seeds from the ground. Only when the covey senses that a predator—a hawk or coyote—has detected it and is about to pounce do the birds take wing.

Colors deepen as the sun sets, the sky gradually becoming pink, the desert itself a golden landscape, beautiful and—for the moment—serene. A delicate sound, like that of a crystal bell in a zephyr, tinkles across the desert: a vermilion flycatcher which has spent the day snapping up flies, gnats, and other insects in the hot sunlight. Now, as evening draws

By day the tarantula hides in a silk-lined nest that it builds in rock crevices or debris, but late in the afternoon this two-inch-long spider emerges and moves swiftly across the desert in search of large beetles, its favorite food.

At the end of the day, a full
moon rises in the pink-washed
sky of the desert at sunset.
The cool air of evening brings
about a stir of animal activity
as the creatures on the
night shift leave their dens and
burrows to begin their nightlong
quest for food and water.

Sweeping in for a landing on a desert shrub, a Gila
woodpecker continues its daylong hunt for food.
It may vary its customary diet of insects with cactus
fruits or an occasional lizard. Unlike many seed-eating
birds, it generally consumes foods that are moist and juicy
and so has little need for drinking water.

upon the desert, the flycatcher begins to sing, rising into the air with each burst of song.

One by one, then in larger numbers, other birds join the chorus. A mockingbird launches its unbroken, ever-varying serenade. A crissal thrasher sings from a perch in the mesquite. The Gila woodpecker redoubles its shrieking in the willows and flies back and forth with even more vigor than it did at noon.

The cool of evening

Now more animals are on the move. For most the goal is food and water. After the parching heat of the day, water comes first, and the water hole—a spring or stream—becomes a center of activity.

Although, as we shall see, some desert animals can get along on surprisingly little water, for many others a good drink of water once or twice a day is a matter of survival.

Think of it as a kind of bondage. All living things must have at least some water. In the forest, where there are many sources of water, this bondage is usually not a hardship. But in the desert, where a single water hole may serve a wide area, the bondage is a primary factor of life for many animals. They dare not venture far from their water hole, even though other considerations, such as food or shelter, might make a long journey desirable.

In the Arizona desert this water bondage is a matter not only of space but also of time. The extreme temperatures of the desert bind the animals to a strict schedule for drinking and foraging. They cannot move about in the open during the day because it is too hot; and many of them cannot move about in the open at night because it is too cold. Consequently they must drink and eat during the few hours of evening and early morning when the temperatures are in-between. This means they have precious little time in which to satisfy their appetites; they must go at it earnestly if they are to get enough food and water to keep them alive.

Because many desert animals require a drink at least once a day, the water hole makes an excellent observation point for those who wish to study the animals without being seen. All you need is a hiding place—a thicket some yards away, or perhaps a portable screen, or "blind," you can make yourself and camouflage with branches and grasses. Almost any water source will do—a stream or small pond. A particularly

A striped skunk pauses for a drink at a desert water hole before setting out on its nightly prowl. Insects, lizards, rodents, birds' eggs—almost anything— will be the object of its nighttime hunting.

39

good observation spot is at the Arizona–Sonora Desert Museum, ten miles west of Tucson. To display the desert as a working and interrelated community, the museum has arranged a number of exhibits, including several with living animals, water holes, and even an underground chamber where visitors may watch burrowing animals and insects in their subterranean habitat. In such circumstances the relationship between plants, insects, birds, and mammals—the great chain of life—is presented to the visitor a good deal more conveniently than he could find for himself in the desert.

Now evening has closed in. A faint glow lingers on the horizon, prolonging the twilight. No longer must the coyote sit panting beneath the cactus; it has a new outlook entirely. For as soon as the heat of day is past, animals that are the coyote's prey come out of their burrows, nests, thickets, and other hiding places. They are easier to find, easier to catch. To the coyote, consequently, evening means food. And food means practically anything—whether it walks, creeps, flies, or stands still. The coyote hunts for a careless rabbit, or scrabbles after a rat among the rocks, or pounces on a sparrow, or leaps into the water to snatch frogs or fish.

Alert and confident, a coyote approaches an alarmed badger. The coyote ponders the best tactic for assault....

...The badger, undaunted by the size of its foe, begins to bristle as it emerges from the entrance of its burrow....

Not far away a badger may be digging out a gopher for supper. Badgers are marvelous diggers, and hence a real danger to such animals as ground squirrels and prairie dogs, which are otherwise fairly safe in their burrows. The badger's long claws are good weapons as well as good earth-movers, and its teeth are sharp. Pigeon-toed, bowlegged, awkward, the badger doesn't win prizes for its looks, but it has such a reputation for ferocity that it is said no other animal its size will attack it.

Such is the endless chain of who-eats-whom. In the evening it becomes intense. The animals go about the business of hunting with a single-mindedness that at first seems brutal and frightening to many human observers. Yet this is the food chain, the process by which life is sustained, and of course life is what gives the desert much of its beauty— its cactuses and wild flowers; its spectacular paloverde and smoke trees; its hawks, owls, and songbirds; its graceful mammals; and its endless variety of reptiles, especially lizards. All these living things must eat in order to survive and reproduce their kind. Each plant, bird, mammal, and reptile fulfills its obligation as hunter or hunted.

. . . Startled by the badger's awesome ferocity, the coyote backs off. Few animals can subdue a badger.

The hours of darkness

If the desert in some respects seems harsh and cruel, there are nevertheless compensations, many of which come at night. As darkness falls, a cool breeze flows down from the mountains, bringing refreshment to the inhabitants of the desert. The temperature drop is sudden and often extreme. It may fall from 120° at midday to 70° at night. The greatest drop ever recorded in a single day was from 126° to 26° in the Sahara. In many areas the fall in temperature is great enough to create dew from the small amount of moisture in the desert air.

The light fades and the stars appear, a few at first but then thousands—a brilliant display. The air takes on an edge of chill. Your first impulse may be to put on a sweater or jacket. For the animals, too, this nighttime coolness brings about a whole new phase in their activities: each must adjust to a radically different environment.

Some animals, unable to stand the cold, take shelter in burrows, bushes, stumps, caves, or holes in trees and cactuses. The nighttime simply was not made for the chuck-

A screech owl leaves its saguaro nest hole at night to hunt. Acute vision and sensitive hearing enable it to locate mice, insects, small lizards, and other prey in the dark.

Though somewhat rare in the desert, the raccoon lives where there is water. Its tracks are usually seen along permanent streams where it makes nightly journeys in search of crayfish and amphibians.

walla, for example, and in general most reptiles require a temperature of 80° or higher if they are to be comfortable.

On the other hand, night means business for the owl, the kit fox, the wildcat, the skunk, the raccoon, and hundreds of other creatures. If the night was not made for them, they are at least made for it. Their ears catch the slightest sounds in the darkness. Their eyes take in the faintest glimmers of light. Some can probably see better by starlight than you can in the full light of the sun. They are able to detect the movements of rats and mice driven forth from their burrows by hunger. Hunger brings them all out, the big and the small, the predators and the prey.

And so off we go again. But instead of the food chain we saw in the daytime—lizard eats insect, road runner eats lizard —now a different group of animals is at work. Now it is mouse eats grass, owl eats mouse; or rabbit eats grass, fox eats rabbit; or insect eats grass, bat eats insect. Vegetation— grasses, cactuses, the seeds and leaves of other plants—is always at the base of the chain. Without it, all animals would perish in a very short time.

Yet if life depends upon competition, upon who eats

Because of the intense heat of the desert during the day, few animals are active. Birds are among the most conspicuous daytime feeders. Here a vulture rests on a saguaro with a captured ground squirrel, a road runner chases a collared lizard, and a gilded flicker drills for insect larvae. A swallowtail butterfly feeds on prickly-pear nectar while many animals, such as the black-tailed jack rabbit, coyote, and sidewinder, wait out the heat in shady spots.

At night predators and prey are on the move. A screech owl, having slept away the day in a saguaro, now attacks a wood rat. A coyote has captured an unwary black-tailed jack rabbit, and a sidewinder sneaks up on a kangaroo rat. Peccaries forage on tough desert plants, while a spotted bat catches nighttime insects on the wing. Mule deer pause for a drink, and a banded gecko, one of the few nocturnal lizards, feeds on a beetle.

With its diet of prickly-pear fruit, this Cetonid beetle fills a special feeding niche in the desert. It does not compete for food with beetles that feed on animal remains or other insects.

whom, there is another sense in which various species also work together without competition. The shift from day to night in the desert illustrates this clearly. Each species has evolved in such a way that it occupies a *niche* in the desert community without serious competition from other species. For example, on the "day shift" in the desert, hawks are the chief birds of prey, hunting mice and squirrels and other small animals; but on the "night shift," owls take over. Hawks and owls, both predators, can live in the same region comfortably and without competing simply because one works by day and the other by night. The day-shift birds and lizards that live on insects do not compete with the night-shift bats. The day-shift seed-eating birds find their food by sight, while the night-shift seed-eating rodents, such as mice and kangaroo rats, find their food by scent. Among reptiles, the lizards are primarily active during daylight hours, while the snakes come out most abundantly at night —to such an extent, in fact, that until desert travelers began using automobiles with bright headlights thirty years or so ago, some species of desert snakes were virtually unknown. And so many species of desert insects are on the night shift that *entomologists* (scientists who study insects) must do a large part of their collecting after dark with ultraviolet lights.

Voices in the night

Even with artificial lights, however, the ability to explore the desert at night would be sharply limited if one had to depend on eyesight alone. You must use your other sense organs, especially your ears. Listening to the desert's night voices can be a fascinating, and sometimes rather alarming, activity for the amateur naturalist.

Actually, the best way to identify an unknown sound is to capture it on a tape recorder, then replay it at leisure—safe at home, with books and manuals to help you. Recording the sounds of nature is a captivating hobby, and not at all expensive. The simplest recorder will do; the more portable the better. The desert is ordinarily so quiet that special gadgets to cut out unwanted noises are unnecessary. Sometimes, of course, if you are collecting the songs of birds that customarily gather in flocks, you may need to record for half an hour to catch a single pure example of the song; but it is

46

easy enough to edit your tape afterward, erasing the parts you don't want. In time you can build up an impressive library of tapes. Aside from the pleasure of forming a collection, you will learn to recognize many species by their voices alone, with the result that you will be at home on the desert even at night.

You are crouched in your hiding place near a water hole. The familiar terrain of day seems strange in the starlight. Your ears are strained for the slightest sound—the whisper of a batwing, the rustle of a mouse in the grass. Suddenly, sounding as if it were no more than a yard away, a blood-curdling shriek breaks out. Even if you know what has made it, your first response is likely to be cold fear. You freeze; images of specters flash through your mind. In a moment you regain your composure and ask yourself for a reasonable explanation. Is a bobcat nearby? A mountain lion? While you are wondering, the shriek sounds again . . . and again.

One of the first things you will learn is that the shriek which so frightened you near the water hole was made by a small, noisy, harmless bird, the yellow-breasted chat. Its call is frequently—and loudly—heard at night. But other night sounds can be even louder: a chorus of toads in springtime can be deafening.

Speckled with tracks, the sandy bottom of an arroyo records the comings and goings of animals that are active in the desert only in the cooler hours after dark.

Prowling at night

Some animals make no noise, or so little that the best-trained ear cannot detect it. You will need a good light to find such creatures. Often your light will reveal an extraordinary amount of activity.

Those who visit the desert only by day will be largely unaware of the host of plant-eating creatures that forage at night; only the leavings and tracks will be visible. But if you go at night, you will see some of them. Turn your flashlight on a creosote bush. Walking sticks are feeding on the foliage, and weevils, as much as an inch long, are conspicuous. Wild bees visit the blossoms of the evening primrose. Here and there you may also catch a glimpse of small furry animals scurrying away from your light. Wood rats are so numerous that they nest in almost every mesquite bush from Texas to California.

The activity of desert animals at night resembles the nocturnal activities of forest animals in many respects. Thou-

47

The showy flowers of the night-blooming cereus burst
open at dusk and wither the following morning.
Night-flying insects pollinate the fragrant blossoms.
This slender branching cactus survives drought by drawing
on water stored in its beetlike root.

sands of creatures are on the prowl. In the forest they are
night birds, raccoons, beavers, muskrats, and mink, among
others. In the desert the animals are different, yet under cover
of darkness there is the same feverish coming and going. The
animals are busy; the object of their business, *food*.

Make no mistake about it, the desert, in spite of its barren appearance, usually offers plenty for animals to eat.
First there is the vegetation—cactuses, trees, shrubs, herbs,
grasses. An enormous number of plant-eating insects, reptiles, and mammals spend the night cropping, chewing,
grazing, and browsing wherever a bit of green vegetation
can be found. For that matter, it does not have to be green.
Brown, yellow, or red, the roots, the stalks, or the bark will
do almost as well as a green leaf. And the seeds, in season,
may be the best of all.

The plant-eaters are preyed upon by larger animals: wea-
sels, snakes, bats, and others. These in turn are pursued by
the powerful predators at the top of the food chain: hawks
and owls, foxes, mountain lions, and bobcats, to name a few.

Insects

The change from day to night affects *every* form of life in
the desert. Plants, for instance, are now deprived of the sunlight they need to manufacture fresh supplies of food. Some
plants that flower during the day close their petals at night,
but some do just the opposite: over millions of years they
have evolved the ability to open at night, thus taking advantage of night-flying insects as aids in pollination. The
beautiful night-blooming cereus is such a plant. Others are
the evening primrose and the sacred datura, or jimson weed.

Sunlight furnishes the energy that green plants need to make food.
The plant-eating animals, unable to use the sun's energy directly,
obtain their nourishment from plants. Still other animals, the meat-
eaters, feed on plant-eating creatures. In this way the energy of
the sun is passed from plant to animal, each linked to the other
in a food chain.

By gnawing a ring of bark from the base of a twig, the mesquite girdler kills the upper portion, where it lays its eggs. When they hatch, the developing young feed on the dead wood of the fallen twig.

Night-blooming plants usually are white and very fragrant, which helps to attract the insects.

To see what great numbers of desert insects there are, collect them for a night or two at an outdoor electric light. An abundance of flying insects will be attracted. Some, especially the moths, are beautifully marked. One can learn to recognize them easily: the leopard moth with spotted wings; the *Hyphantria*, colored a delicate white; the orange, yellow, and black *Cisthene*; *Pygarctia*, with gray wings and red body; the red-underwing *Catocala*; and one of the most remarkable of the smaller moths, the white *Rhodophora*, marked with purple. The hawk moth, intricately marked and softly colored, sips nectar at an evening primrose, hovering characteristically on rapidly beating wings and then moving backward away from the blossom.

The world of insects is far larger than most people realize. One person could not begin to study all the desert varieties; a lifetime would not afford enough time. So far, in fact, only the surface has been scratched by all desert entomologists working together. Moreover, the daytime insects are quite as remarkable as those of the night, brilliantly colored and strikingly patterned. The scarab beetle and the *Scolia*

Gorged with honeydew in times of plenty, certain
members of honey ant colonies *(left)* become living storage
jars. Swollen to the size of currants, they hang from
the ceilings of underground galleries. When food
grows scarce, all the honey ants feed on the sweet liquid.

wasp are notable examples, along with such butterflies as
the tiger swallowtail and the sulphur.

But although human observers value the insects in part
for their colors, bats and nighthawks and other insect-eating
species care only for food. A bat may consume more than
half its own weight in insects during a single night. Bat
colonies numbering in the thousands will eat enormous numbers of insects every night. More than 1800 winged ants
were found in the stomach of one nighthawk, and 500 mos-
quitoes in another. Such insect-eating species are part of the
intricate system of natural controls that prevents insects
from overrunning the earth.

An inch-long scarab beetle,
Plusiotis, clambers across a sprig
of Arizona juniper. As an adult
it eats nothing, but the larvae
are voracious scavengers that
help build soil.

Diving from above, the
robber fly captures insect
victims, such as wasps, in
midair. Then it carries them
to a convenient perch and sucks
out their body juices.

Lapping nectar with their slender tongues, two long-nosed bats are unknowingly pollinating desert flowers. These nocturnal acrobats probably supplement their liquid diet with insects.

Depending on one another

The insects occupy a twofold position in the life of the desert. First, without insects many cross-pollinated plants would disappear. Indeed, the yuccas, such as the Spanish dagger and the Joshua tree, are completely dependent upon the small moth *Tegeticula* which pollinates them. Second, without insects there would be no insectivorous bats and nighthawks. Insects bring life to bats and nighthawks by furnishing them food, and to plants by pollinating them and thus enabling them to reproduce. Many other species of birds and mammals and reptiles are insect-eaters as well.

But suppose for a moment that the desert's insects vanished and the plants remained unpollinated, for example a plant like the giant saguaro cactus. Gradually over fifty years or longer the saguaros would die off without any new ones to replace them. This would mean a loss of nesting places for many owls. As owls decreased in numbers, the seed-eating rats and mice would increase until they would be eating all the seeds the other desert plants could produce. This would mean a sharp decrease of vegetation and an increase in wind erosion. As a result the desert would become more and more barren, and in time all life might disappear from it.

This is an oversimplification, of course. Many other things might happen. For instance, when the owls decreased and the mice increased, perhaps the kit foxes would also increase, finding more mice to feed upon. Even without the owls, then, the balance between seeds and seed-eaters might not be upset. Thousands of other factors might also be involved, but this is the point: Nature is an immense system of interrelationships involving so many factors that man cannot take them all into account. That is why some of man's experiments to control nature, such as the massive campaigns to destroy insects with chemicals, have backfired. Some unforeseen results of these campaigns have been more harmful than the original pests they were designed to destroy.

Yucca moths lay their eggs at the base of yucca blossoms and then pollinate them by stuffing pollen in the flower pistils. The moth caterpillars hatch inside the fruit, eat a few seeds, and then emerge as adults. Both moth and yucca benefit from the partnership: the moth caterpillar has food, and the yucca is pollinated.

Underground, another level of life carries on its work largely unseen, though its contribution to the whole is essential. Burrowing mammals, such as pocket gophers, and smaller creatures, such as ants and lizards, continually move the soil as they construct their homes, and often the ground is threaded with their burrows. Their work is extremely important in loosening the soil so that air and water can enter it easily. Without them, in some places the ground would become so hard-packed that no plants would find a roothold.

Paul B. Sears, a famous botanist, once said that the face of the earth has always been a graveyard: all living things return to the soil whatever they have taken from it. The leaves of a tree rot on the ground in the winter and enrich the soil. Thus the trees return part of the nutrients they have taken from the ground in summer. All plants die and return to the earth, and so do all animals. Endlessly they are broken down into nitrates, phosphates, and other chemical compounds on which all life is dependent. These compounds are taken from the soil and returned to it over and over again.

In other words, the *habitat* is replenished. By habitat we mean the soil, rocks, climate, water—everything necessary to life in a particular location. Life is said to arise and flourish in a certain habitat. Life gets the substances it needs from the habitat. If the habitat is not replenished, the life that exists in it will die—first the plants, then the animals. Yet the only way, generally speaking, in which a certain habitat may be replenished is through the continual return of the substances that have been taken from it. Thus the cycle of life and death is kept going not only through life's ability to reproduce itself, but also through the earth's ability to reabsorb the essential substances released in death. When this cycle is broken, the consequences may be very serious indeed.

The nighttime prowl continues. You may be tempted to stay on the highway, where the pavement retains the day-

The complex interrelationships between living things in the desert, as everywhere, depend on green plants, or producers, that manufacture food from carbon dioxide, water, and the energy of sunlight. First-order consumers feed directly on plants. Second-order consumers eat first-order consumers. Third-order consumers obtain nourishment from first- and second-order consumers and green plants. Ultimately producers and consumers die, and decomposers break them down into chemical compounds necessary for new plant growth.

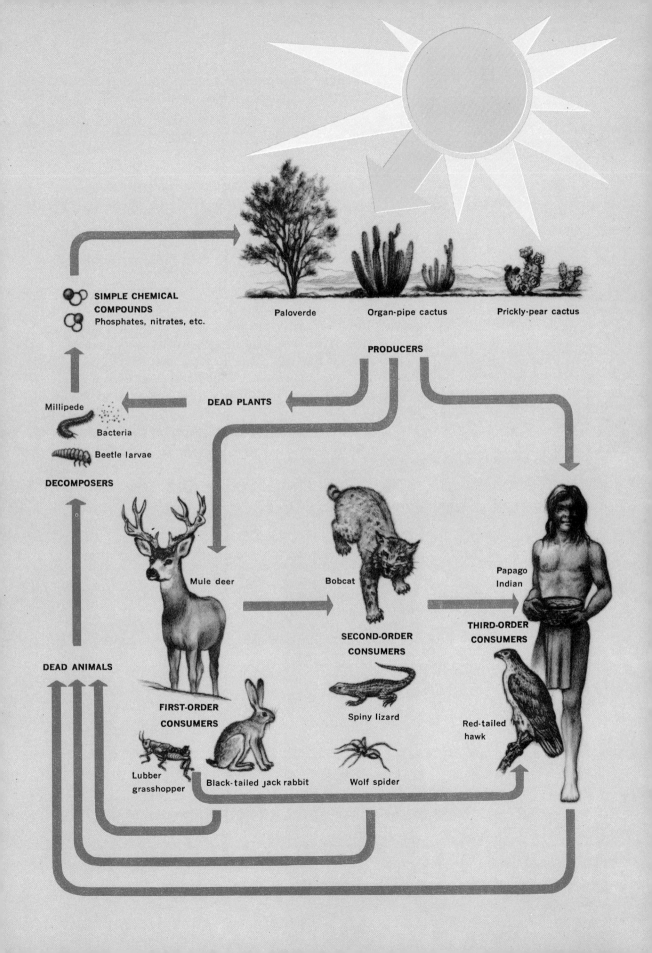

SIMPLE CHEMICAL
COMPOUNDS
Phosphates, nitrates, etc.

Paloverde

Organ-pipe cactus

Prickly-pear cactus

PRODUCERS

DEAD PLANTS

Millipede

Bacteria

Beetle larvae

DECOMPOSERS

Mule deer

Bobcat

Papago
Indian

THIRD-ORDER
CONSUMERS

SECOND-ORDER
CONSUMERS

DEAD ANIMALS

FIRST-ORDER
CONSUMERS

Spiny lizard

Red-tailed
hawk

Lubber
grasshopper

Black-tailed jack rabbit

Wolf spider

time heat longer than the surrounding soil. Many reptiles, especially snakes, seek this lingering warmth, and on the highway they are relatively easy to see and capture.

Nevertheless, you must leave the pavement if you wish to find the "pure" communities of plants and animals that characterize the desert. What you are looking for—if you are interested in the really exciting part of desert exploration—is an area in which all elements of a natural community exist in balance, as they existed before the coming of man's mechanized civilization. The plants and animals, including man himself as a single integrated element rather than the overlord, all living in a coordinated natural system: this is what you wish to see. Probably there is no place in the United States where you can any longer find it, no place where the earth and climate have not been altered at least a little by man's enterprises or where all the original species survive intact. The genuine wilderness in the United States, whether desert, grassland, or forest, has been greatly reduced.

Yet you can come fairly close to genuine wilderness in some areas that have been protected against the attacks of the machine. Most such places are parklands. The largest

Like stiff grass skirts, tiers of dead leaves thatch the trunks of Spanish daggers. These unusual yuccas are especially plentiful at Big Bend National Park, Texas, where they often grow as high as twenty-five feet.

are the great preserves of the federal and state governments, but there is also a good number of smaller wildlife preserves owned by such private organizations as the National Audubon Society and the Nature Conservancy. Altogether these make up a reasonably inclusive system of parks, ranging from the subtropical forests of Florida to the great fir forests of the North. Other parks contain tracts of shorelines, prairies, mountains, swamps, rivers, and—of special interest to us—deserts. True, none of these parks gives us the desert as it was two thousand years ago. Numerous species have been reduced in numbers, particularly predatory animals. But enough still remain for the trained observer to be able to imagine what the primeval desert was like.

One of the largest desert preserves is Big Bend National Park, established in 1944. It encloses more than 708,000 acres located within a huge bend of the Rio Grande on the Texas–Mexico frontier, a part of the Chihuahuan Desert. Since 1944, when the grazing of cattle and sheep on this land was stopped, the vegetation has made a comeback, with broad stretches of lechuguilla and sotol that characterize the lowlands. In addition, the park includes rugged mountains, high plateaus, and canyons whose depths are lost in shadow—some of the most striking desert vistas in the United States. Large yuccas called Spanish daggers bloom profusely, raising great white clusters of blossoms toward the sky.

Other important desert units of the National Park System are Saguaro, Organ Pipe Cactus, Joshua Tree, and White Sands National Monuments, all established in the 1930s. California has set aside the Anza–Borrego State Park in an area that includes both desert and mountains. All these parks, and others, are extremely important to American desert scientists, who would have no "natural laboratory" if the parks did not exist; but the parks are equally important to anyone who wishes to see what the desert is really like.

The Joshua tree's strange branching form results from its tendency to grow in a new direction wherever a blossom cluster forms. Forests of these bizarre tree yuccas are the chief attraction of Joshua Tree National Monument, California.

Dawn

The first light seeps over the horizon, silvery and cold. The stars fade. It is a quiet, almost uncanny time, the coldest part of the desert day. The heat of yesterday, stored in rocks and sand during the night, has almost entirely dissipated. Everything is still. The cold-blooded snakes, toads, and lizards have buried themselves in the sand or crept into holes and crevices.

White-winged doves surround a desert water hole at dawn.

Yet the stillness is never quite complete. The predawn serenity is broken by a sound like a half-muffled burst of machine-gun fire; it is enough to bring any sleeper scrambling from his sleeping bag, but this is merely the "song" of a cactus wren, perched atop the tallest saguaro in the area.

Now the desert comes to life quickly. Doves coo. Mockingbirds begin to sing. The quail are up, heading toward the water hole, chattering all the way. The Gila woodpecker once again swoops noisily among the sycamores.

Birds are the desert's early risers; they can withstand the cold dawn. They are up and busy, gathering food. Not so the reptiles. Their bodies cannot regulate heat internally as effectively as the warm-blooded animals can, so they must wait until the surroundings warm up before they venture forth. Spotted whiptails and spiny lizards and their brethren are seldom seen until they are warm enough to move about easily.

Warm-blooded animals are not held so strictly in this temperature bondage. They are on the move early. The deer that came down to the lowlands for water and warmth during the night now slip back to the upper ranges. Coyotes and foxes prowl through the mesquite, on the lookout for a last tidbit before the heat of day forces them once more into inactivity. Bands of javelina (the only native wild pig in the United States) search for prickly-pear fruit among the cactuses.

Although it is more active at night, the gray fox is occasionally seen by day in desert mountains, foothills, and canyons. Rabbits comprise more than 30 per cent of its diet.

Sunrise

The sun breaks between distant peaks. Long shadows of saguaros stretch across the desert. Now is the time to get going. If your camp is in the wild desert, remove or destroy every evidence of your campsite. If it is a public campground, make it ready for the next occupant by restoring it to good order and cleanliness.

Public campgrounds often serve admirably as base camps from which to conduct sunrise expeditions. Many are so located as to offer a variety of terrain. One morning you may

The long shadows of giant saguaros stretch across the desert floor at daybreak. Night prowlers slip noiselessly into their dens and burrows, while many birds, lizards, and other daytime animals emerge from hiding and begin another feeding shift throughout the desert.

head for the high desert country, the next for the lowlands, the next for a remote canyon. In each case the morning hours will give you good light and a comfortable temperature, if you get started early enough. Then you can return to camp to spend the hot afternoon in the shade.

You set off. There goes a road runner after a lizard! Does it seem familiar? Of course. The daytime food chains are being re-established. The community of wild creatures is changing shifts again, as dependably as the rising of the sun. There is almost frenzied activity as the animals begin the day's operations, as if they had only an hour or two to live. They do have few enough hours of coolness left in which to satisfy thirst and hunger.

Millions of suns have risen and set as these animals have come, by the slow process of evolution, to react instinctively to desert extremes of day and night, heat and cold. Now they do their work as automatically as machines responding to the commands of the sun. Periods of intense activity alternate with periods of repose according to the strict schedule of temperature, and the animals themselves are probably

A desert crested lizard pauses in the shade of a rock as the heat of day soars upward. This hardy vegetarian can thrive even on the tough leaves of creosote bush.

unaware of their changing momentum. Now they throng to the water hole. At dawn there can be no question about the role water plays in their movements. A few escape water bondage; but most must find water every morning or suffer during the hot day ahead.

The order of night quickly gives place to the order of day. Shadows shorten. The golden light of dawn turns to yellow, then to the bright white light of day. Night-wandering animals cease wandering and seek their homes: the owl to its roost or burrow, the bat to its cave. A mother raccoon leads her young down to the water's edge for a bedtime drink. Ringtails and kit foxes retire for the day into their holes. Kangaroo rats withdraw to cooler and safer quarters underground. The night-blooming flowers close their petals, and the colorful moths cling to the undersides of leaves, where they will hang, wings folded, drab and unnoticed, all day.

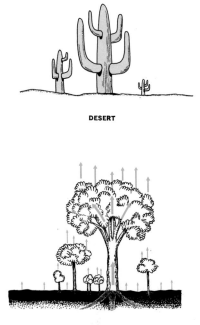

DESERT

FOREST

Daily rhythm

Now the sun climbs higher, and the air begins to heat. The sun's energy drenches everything, pouring onto the plants, the sand and rock. If dew has collected on grasses and leaves, it evaporates quickly. The relative humidity, which may have risen as high as 100 per cent during the night, now drops abruptly to 20 per cent or less. You are once again subjected to the extreme dryness and heat of the desert in daytime.

The daytime community resumes its activities; or rather, its inactivities. As the heat increases, the quail disappear into the shade, and the coyote seeks a resting place. The glare of light increases until human vision blurs. The Gila woodpecker remains lively, swooping and shrieking among the sycamores.

The change during your twenty-four hours on the desert has been more extreme than you could find in any other natural habitat. During one day and night the temperature has dropped perhaps as much as eighty degrees and risen again—more than twice the average temperature variation in the United States. Whole groups of night-blooming plants have opened their petals in the dark, unseen except by moths and other night-flying insects, and now at midday the petals have withered. Night-prowling animals have emerged

In deserts there is little water available to evaporate and carry off heat. Most of the sun's energy goes into heating up soil surfaces. The ground is dry, and the desert plants and animals hoard whatever water they collect, transpiring and perspiring very little. In forests, however, there is an abundance of water. Much of the sun's energy goes into evaporating water rather than into raising surface temperatures. Wherever sunlight strikes leaves or damp soil, heat is quickly carried off in the vapor of evaporating water. Indeed, more than 2500 gallons of water may evaporate from an acre of forest in just one day.

from their caves and burrows, then returned to them, their hunger and thirst satisfied. Snakes, lizards, and toads have fled, first from the heat, then from the cold, in an endless escape from extreme temperatures. The difference between day and night in the desert is as great as the difference between summer and winter in many parts of the world.

The entire life of the desert—every mammal, reptile, insect, bird, and plant—has evolved in such a way that it can cope with this extreme cycle of temperature. Plants, unable to move from the places where they are rooted, have survived through internal changes, as we shall see later. Animals have experienced an entire cycle of behavior, from intense activity to torpor. Considered as a single huge mechanism, the desert has functioned throughout the twenty-four hours with almost unbelievable precision and intricacy, according to a pattern that has developed over millions of years. Each separate part of the mechanism has played its role.

The day mounts toward its hottest hour. Stillness returns. The chorus of morning birdsong subsides and the coyotes retire. Not a breath of life appears to stir in this stifling, hot land. The arms of the giant saguaro cactuses seem to reach toward the sky in a plea for life-giving water. Once more the sun has reached its zenith, and the desert lies scorched and burning.

Two by two, the footprints of a coyote trace its course across the burning sands of a desert dune. The coyote, like many other desert animals, has retreated to a shady spot to await the cooler air of nighttime, when it will once again start out in search of life-giving food.

The Desert Wet and Dry

SUMMER BEGINS—May, June, the first burning days of July. A few traces of moisture appear in the desert air. At first they are almost nothing; visitors from other areas hardly notice them—white wisps of cloud drifting along the peaks of the horizon, far away. But those who live in the desert know what they mean.

The wispy clouds floating on the horizon move quickly, then disappear, leaving the desert sky as blue and dry as ever. The next day they come again, and again they disappear. Somewhere beyond the mountains, moist air masses from the distant sea are crowding against the hot, dry air of the desert.

Day by day the small clouds come and go. Now you see them, now you don't. They may appear at any time—morning, afternoon, or evening. Old-timers in the desert say they make their appearance toward the end of June and then by the Fourth of July the rain begins. Often the old-timers are right.

The beginning is a bang. About mid-morning the clouds start piling up. Small white wispy clouds rise above the mountains. In less than an hour they have mushroomed into

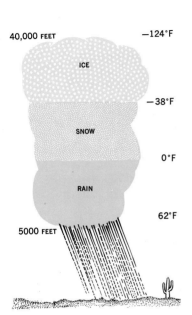

40,000 FEET   −124°F

ICE

−38°F

SNOW

0°F

RAIN

62°F

5000 FEET

A fully developed thunderhead may be as much as 40,000 feet high at its top. The temperatures within the cloud vary so greatly that layers of rain, snow, and ice crystals are formed. Strong updrafts hold these within the cloud until they become so heavy that they begin to fall. Then the updrafts are turned into downdrafts. A cold, heavy downpour, accompanied by high winds, results.

a huge mass, and by noon they have grown so vast that their shadows darken the peaks below. Inside them, violent dark billows roll in and out like smoke above a volcano. Minute by minute the hot air of the desert rises into the cool air coming across the mountains at elevations of 5000 feet or more; the sudden mixing creates turbulent masses containing billions of droplets of water. The result is a cumulonimbus cloud (from *cumulus,* meaning heap, and *nimbus,* cloud), commonly called a *thunderhead.*

Thunderheads are known almost everywhere; they are the clouds that make summer thunderstorms. But in the desert, where the contrast between hot surface air and cold upper air is greater than in most other places, the thunderhead is especially dramatic. Inside it, swift updrafts and downdrafts churn violently, so that an airplane flying into it would be tossed about like a feather. In addition, these conflicting currents carry water droplets, dust, and other particles that brush together and collide, causing friction. The result is a swift build-up of static electricity.

The storm strikes with a warning rumble. Scarcely more than two hours after the first wisps appeared above the peak, the storm has begun. A flash of lightning leaps in the sky, illuminating the interior of the cloud like a Chinese lantern. A roar of thunder rolls over the cliffs and booms across the flats. The wind rises—a cool wind from the mountains, strange and unfamiliar in the midday heat. Little puffs of dust dance before it. A few minutes earlier the birds and other animals had been settling into their midday repose. Now they are suddenly on the move: birds flying and singing, or flitting back and forth among the creosote bushes; cottontails and other small creatures running uncertainly, as if the accustomed pattern of their world were being upset.

It is. Where before the desert was brilliant in the glare of sunlight, now it is dark. Where the sky was blue and blindingly bright, clouds now shut out the sun. Swirls of dust run like elfin figures along the flats and washes. The branches of willows and sycamores wave in the wind.

The race for shelter

More lightning, more thunder. The reverberations seem to shake the desert's foundations. The inhabitants of the desert head for cover—scurrying, swooping, darting, running, flying in all directions. They seek whatever protection they can find—the nearest crevice, the closest bush. Perhaps the birds are the luckiest, elf owls, woodpeckers, martins, and others that live in holes aboveground; they are safe so long as their tree or cactus doesn't snap off in the wind. Reptiles and burrowing mammals scoot into underground passages, obeying their instinct to go into the earth. There they are secure against the ravages of wind. But what about water? Many a gopher has drowned in its burrow. The larger animals run to the shelter of a hollow beneath an overhanging rock or in a dense thicket of mesquite.

Lightning cracks across the sky, illuminating the now-greenish undersides of the clouds; thunder rattles and bangs; the wind rises in gusts, veering and whirling. Then the rain begins, drop by drop at first, then two at a time—huge drops

A shaft of rain falls from a distant rain cloud as a summer rainstorm crosses the Arizona desert. The winds accompanying such storms sometimes are strong enough to topple even sturdy saguaro cactuses.

that spatter on the rocks and raise little puffs of dust. Quickly the rain increases until the whole fury of the storm is unleashed. The downpour is so heavy that it seems as if the air were entirely replaced by rain.

But look around you on the horizon. Another thunderhead has risen, and another. Separate storms have developed around the entire rim of the desert, and now they are all under way at once. At the height of the rainy season, a visitor may stand at a vantage point, such as the North Rim of the Grand Canyon in Arizona, and see a dozen thunderstorms in progress at once, some beginning, some rising into immense thunderheads, some pouring black curtains of rain, some disappearing on the eastern horizon.

Flash flood

For plants and animals a storm is a matter of life and death: life because the rain ends months of drought; death because winds and floods leave havoc in their wake.

Lightning, too, is a paradox of the storm. Death by electrocution is not uncommon among desert animals, yet at the same time lightning is also important to the life of the desert, as to all life everywhere. Lightning passing through the atmosphere combines atmospheric nitrogen (nearly eight-tenths of the earth's atmosphere) with oxygen, forming compounds that fall to the ground with other nitrogen compounds dissolved in rain and snow. Lightning thus helps to convert nitrogen to a form that can be used by living things. The nitrogen produced by soil microbes together with the nitrogen from the air pass from the soil to the plants to the plant-eating animals and to the flesh-eating animals through the food chain. In fact, nitrogen is a part of all living tissues. When a plant or animal dies, the nitrogen is returned to the soil and again becomes available for use by plants.

As the storm breaks, rain falls in a torrent. Immediately little rivulets form on the ground, snaking in and out among rocks and plants. The rivulets join; cascades roll across the slopes; sheets of water gather in the flats. In two minutes half-grown rivers are bolting across the desert floor. They reach the *arroyo*, a dry channel that has not carried water for months. Whitecapped, turbulent, and muddy, the water stampedes down the arroyo, sweeping everything before it.

A coyote, soaked and draggle-tailed, dashes for a cleft in

A muddy torrent of water from a desert cloudburst rushes down the channel of an arroyo. Within an hour or two the seething waters may subside to a trickle.

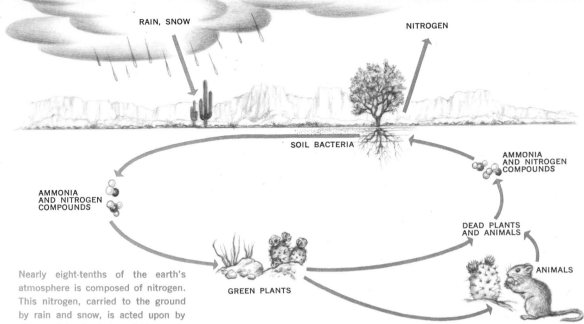

RAIN, SNOW

NITROGEN

SOIL BACTERIA

AMMONIA AND NITROGEN COMPOUNDS

AMMONIA AND NITROGEN COMPOUNDS

DEAD PLANTS AND ANIMALS

GREEN PLANTS

ANIMALS

Nearly eight-tenths of the earth's atmosphere is composed of nitrogen. This nitrogen, carried to the ground by rain and snow, is acted upon by nitrogen-fixing bacteria and blue-green algae that combine it with oxygen and hydrogen. In turn, these compounds are used by green plants and are passed on to plant-eating animals. The meat-eating animals get their nitrogen by eating plant-eaters. When plants and animals die, they are broken down by decay organisms into ammonia and nitrogen compounds once again. Some of the nitrogen returns to the atmosphere, but some is used again by green plants, and the cycle begins anew.

the rock. Its shelter under a buckthorn thicket has proved inadequate. With the intelligence of all its species, the coyote knows just the place among the rocks that will give it the best security against the storm.

As the storm intensifies, hail may fall. In a few seconds the floor of the desert may be covered with white hailstones. The driving stones tear the leaves off trees and puncture the tough skins of the cactuses. The jack rabbit cowers in its shelter, and the Gila woodpecker for once sits quietly in its hole. Insects fold their wings tightly, clinging to stems and twigs.

By now the flash flood is at its height. Water plunging down the arroyo uproots trees and tears away bushes along the banks, carrying tons of sand, gravel, and even large stones. As the torrent swells and the burden of debris increases, the damage done by the flood becomes worse and worse, scarring the banks and anything that grows there. Large sections of land may be swept away, with dry, powdery earth subsiding into the torrent like a pinch of salt in a boiling pot. And when the land caves in, any animals living there go with it. Rats, mice, and rabbits try vainly to swim in the seething waters. Beetles, wasps, lizards, and rattlesnakes go sweeping by, struggling desperately or perhaps already dead.

Human beings also may experience the water's peril. Unwary visitors to the desert have been caught often enough in flash floods. In many desert areas today you see roadside signs that read DIP, which signifies a low place in the highway. Sometimes these low places are natural depressions; sometimes they are made by road builders to permit a flood to cross the highway without destroying it. The experienced desert traveler seldom crosses a dip if there is water in it, and he will hurry across in any case, especially if there is the slightest sign of rain. A car stalled in a dip can be washed away in an instant when a flash flood comes surging down it.

Desert floods are responsible for one of the most noticeable features of desert scenery, the *alluvial fan*. Flooded rivers roll down the mountains onto the desert floor, where they spread out in all directions. Earth and stones brought down by the flood are left in a fan-shaped pattern on the desert floor, particularly visible from the air since the flood-carried sediment is usually of a color different from that of the surrounding soil. At the same time, fan-shaped patterns

The rushing water of desert flash floods often collects in natural basins, forming temporary playa lakes. These quick-drying lakes are only a few inches deep but may cover hundreds of acres. They are so salty that only a few tough plants, such as saltbush and pickleweed, are able to grow in them.

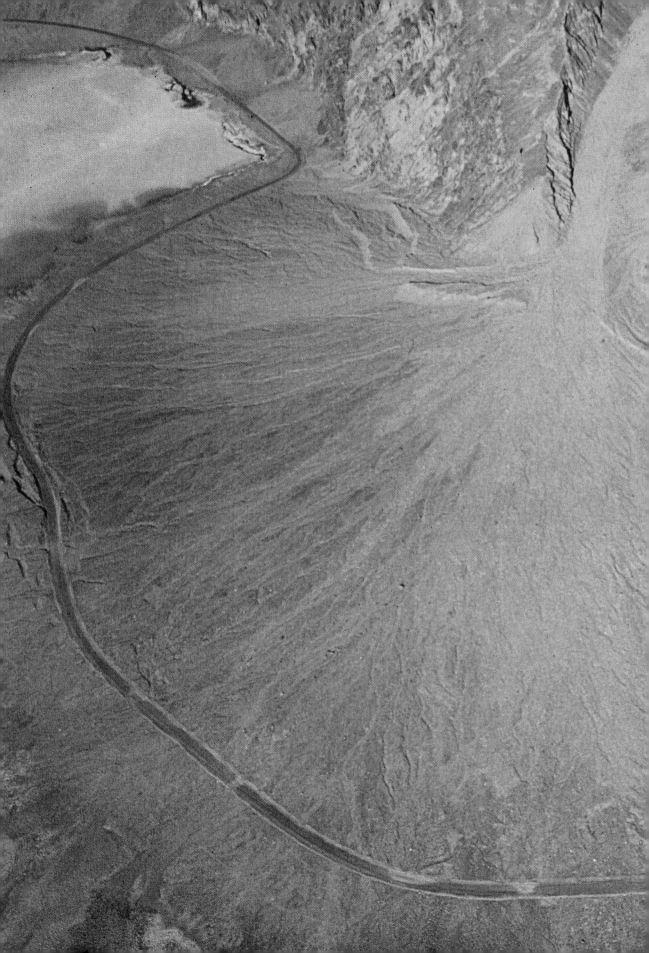

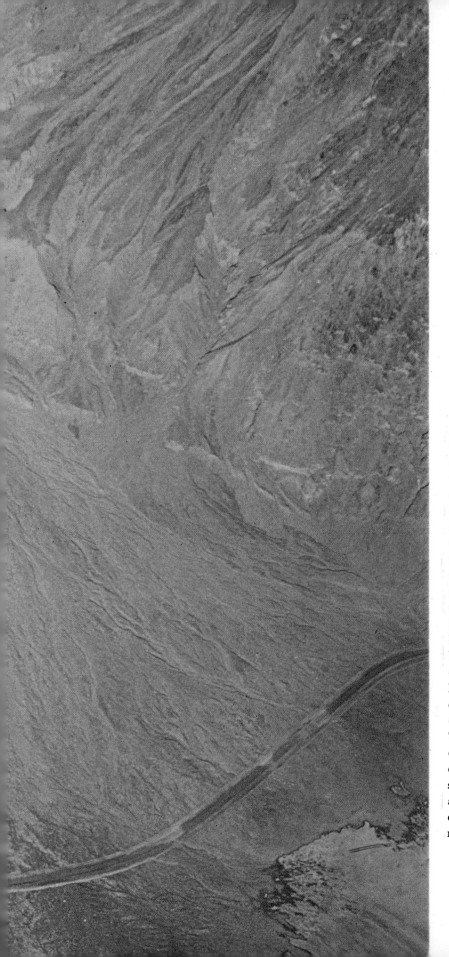

Alluvial fans are formed when water rushing down a steep channel is slowed by the flat valley floor below it. Water moving at great speed can carry a large load of silt, sand, and rock, but slow-moving water cannot. As a result, when the water slows down, a fan of water-carried debris is dumped at the base of the channel where it meets level land. Each flash flood sends new material hurtling down the channel, but between storms erosion fills in old stream routes over the fan. Because of this, the stream crosses the fan in a new direction each time it rains. The fan is thus enlarged first on one side and then on the other, in a remarkably symmetrical way. It is actually a series of many smaller fans, each the result of a different rainstorm.

The extensive prairie-dog "towns" that once were common in many areas of the desert have been seriously reduced by man. Prairie-dog burrows not only help to conserve rain water but also offer ready-made homes to burrowing owls and desert snakes.

Not only does the badger construct burrows in which to live, it also uses its sharp two-inch-long claws to dig out ground squirrels, thereby loosening hard-packed desert soil and making it possible for plants to flourish.

of vegetation may spring up on the bottom land, since floods often bring down seeds originally deposited at higher elevations. Thus the natural course of floodwaters can be traced with ease, even in times of dryness.

Water, water everywhere

You might suppose the dry desert soil would soak up rainfall like blotting paper. Just the opposite. First, the rain falls faster than the ground can absorb it. Second, the earth of the desert is not like blotting paper at all; it resembles city pavement. The earthworms that are so important in making soil loose and spongy in other areas are virtually nonexistent in the desert. At the same time the burrowing animals of the desert that might contribute to soil-mixing—including prairie dogs, pocket gophers, and badgers—in many areas have been largely eliminated by rodent-control programs. Extermination, not "control," is the goal of many such programs, and nothing could be more harmful to the desert. The good done by burrowing animals in stirring up the earth and providing underground passages for moisture far exceeds the damage they inflict.

Other factors are also at work. Forests and grasslands have an abundance of dead grasses, leaves, and fallen branches continuously decaying on the surface. This makes a spongy layer of material to hold the water. Nothing like this happens on the desert, where the plants are too sparse to furnish much decaying vegetable matter. The result is that desert winds blow away any dead leaves that fall, along with the soil itself, leaving only a hard-packed, stony "desert pavement."

It is a vicious circle. Because desert vegetation is sparse, there are few dense deposits of decaying vegetable matter to capture the rainfall, and hence the soil is hard-packed. Because the soil is hard-packed, the rainfall runs off easily, and the soil remains dry. Because the soil is dry, plant growth remains sparse.

In certain parts of the desert the total rainfall for a whole year may fall in a single intense downpour. Desert explorers know that an inch of rainfall in ten minutes is not unusual, though government weather stations are so widely scattered in the desert that reliable statistics are scanty. The point to remember is that desert storms can be swift and terrible, leaving the land both shattered and refreshed.

The sky lightens, the pounding rain slackens. The raindrops thin out and become smaller, until they turn into

Where the ground squirrel has been able to escape the rodent-control programs of man, it continues to carry on the valuable job of soil-mixing. At the same time, its extensive network of underground tunnels is an effective trap for rain water.

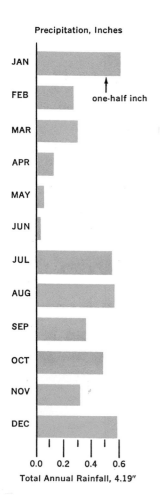

Precipitation, Inches

JAN	
FEB	↑ one-half inch
MAR	
APR	
MAY	
JUN	
JUL	
AUG	
SEP	
OCT	
NOV	
DEC	

0.0   0.2   0.4   0.6

Total Annual Rainfall, 4.19″

This graph shows the annual rainfall at Twentynine Palms, California, near the northern edge of Joshua Tree National Monument. It illustrates that the Arizona desert has two distinct rainy seasons, one in July and August, another in December and January.

drizzle. The coyote emerges from its shelter shaking its coat, and the Gila woodpecker explodes from its hole as if catapulted by a spring. Insects crawl onto the upper surfaces of stems and leaves, drying their wings with their legs. At last the sun breaks through.

Sunlight descends in single rays at first, luminous beams slanting through the overcast. Mist rises in billows. The torrent in the arroyo rages without letup, but the rivulets among rocks and thickets quickly become small trickles and then cease altogether. The sound of water dripping from rocks and branches fills the desert. It has been perhaps half an hour since the first raindrops fell, and it will be another hour before the muddy deluge in the arroyo begins to subside. Several days may pass before the final trickle gives out.

Of course another storm may come tomorrow, a repetition of the violence and flooding. Not all parts of the desert must get along on one storm a year. The summer rainy season in the Southwest usually lasts for only a few weeks, with daily cloudbursts that sometimes continue into August. A second rainy season begins in December and continues through January. But thunderstorms, no matter when they occur, are small in extent; the part of the desert actually covered by a single thunderstorm may be no more than a few square miles. Any particular location may receive rainfall only a few times a year, even though a relatively large number of thunderstorms pass through the general area.

The storm is over, the sun has come out, and the sky is blue. But nearer the ground mist rises thickly, almost like steam, and even though the sunlight is as intense as ever, much of the sun's energy is now absorbed by this unusual humidity. Consequently the desert afternoon is cooler and more pleasant than is usual. With water everywhere—pools of it, rivers of it—the animals are no longer so restricted in their movements; they can go farther afield in their search for food and mates, and so there is a great dispersal of creatures ordinarily dependent on isolated water holes. An unusual stir and excitement fills the desert, and everywhere, in all directions, birdsongs fill the air.

Miracle in the desert

Almost overnight one of nature's miracles takes place. In puddles and lakes left from the storm, tiny shrimp appear—

78

as if they had come from nowhere or had fallen with the rain from the sky. They are fresh-water species called brine shrimp, tadpole shrimp, and fairy shrimp, rather different from the ocean species favored by seafood lovers, yet sufficiently shrimplike to be recognizable. They have hatched from eggs deposited in the soil years before, whenever the last puddle formed in the same spot. There are records of desert shrimp hatching where there has been no water for twenty-five years, and scientists believe that shrimp eggs may hatch successfully after as much as a century of lying dormant. It seems incredible, yet there they are: the puddle is bursting with life. But the puddle will not last long; the shrimp must live in a hurry. In fact, their life cycle is so compressed that growth, mating, and the laying of new eggs are completed before the puddle dries up. When the water is gone, the new eggs will lie in the sand, living but dormant, until water comes again.

In previous geologic eras the West was under water. Sometimes the deserts were ocean beds, sometimes they were covered by fresh-water lakes or swamps. The desert shrimp perhaps are living relics of those ancient times. As the desert became drier, the shrimp became adjusted gradually to their new conditions of life. Finally they evolved into their present form, probably (from the point of view of mere survival) the most perfectly adjusted of all desert creatures. From the point of view of evolutionary progress, though, desert shrimp remain a rather primitive species.

The tadpole shrimp (*above*) lives out its short life in temporary pools formed by desert rainstorms. Hatching from an egg as soon as the water collects, it must then reach adulthood, mate, and lay new eggs before the pool dries up. When the water is gone, the adult shrimps are left stranded and dead in the mud (*below*).

Spurred into action by rain, a spadefoot toad pushes up through the sand. . . .

. . . On the surface, the toad rubs the sand from its eyes with its hind foot. . . .

Other creatures, too, take advantage of the gift of water. Spadefoot toads are a good example. They get their name from their spadelike hind feet, with which they dig themselves into the sand; they go in backward, and can disappear in a few seconds. During the hottest, driest weather, the spadefoot spends a good deal of time buried beneath the surface of the ground, coming out only at night to hunt insects. But the coming of rain signals a change in its behavior: it is the time for mating. Soon after the rain has gone, you can find clusters of spadefoot eggs in the temporary pools of water that remain; within two or three days tadpoles appear, as many as 200 from a single cluster; they in turn are transformed into toads in about four to six weeks. Other species of toads, living in regions where water is more abundant, may require two months for the transformation from tadpole to adult.

Similarly, in some desert areas the mating and nesting of birds occurs at times of rain, rather than automatically each spring. In North Africa and Australia scientists have found that desert birds will even migrate from rainless areas to places where rain has fallen, perhaps because the female birds need more water than usual when laying eggs. Often the nests are built and eggs are laid within a week after the rain has come. The same fast-moving life processes can be observed among many desert animals when the infrequent rains bring relief from heat and dryness.

But nothing in the animal world is so spectacular as the show put on by plants. For months, maybe even years, the seeds of flowering plants have been blown about by desert winds or have lain dormant in the soil. Some seeds may lie dormant in the sand for many years, although obviously this is a difficult thing to measure. Scientists are uncertain how long a seed can remain alive in the extreme heat and dryness of the desert.

The rain comes at last. The hulls of the seeds are moistened. Somewhere inside, the spark of life is stimulated, and a new plant comes into being. Almost overnight the desert floor becomes a paradise of color. As far as the eye can see a carpet of blossoms spreads: poppies, primroses, mallows, bee plants, zinnias, four-o'clocks, and others. In some places the display may seem almost solid, in others the plants are more scattered. But in either case the beauty of desert

. . . Sitting absolutely motionless, the spadefoot waits for an unwary insect to pass its way. . . .

. . . With a flick of its sticky tongue the toad captures an insect larva. Once its feeding is over, the toad will again bury itself in the sand and wait out the hotter hours.

flowers is one of nature's truly impressive spectacles. Indeed, the desert flower blooming unseen in remote wastes has been a popular image for poets since the beginning of civilization.

Whatever it is that keeps desert seeds from sprouting at times of dryness is certainly not an accident. A seed that began to grow without any prospect of water would wither and die almost immediately.

Less than 1 per cent of desert annual wild-flower seeds germinate after a brief rainstorm, whereas a heavy rainstorm causes more than 50 per cent of the seeds to sprout. The reason for this is simple. A seed must not only germinate but must also grow to maturity in order to produce new seeds and ensure the survival of the species. A plant that sprouts after a brief rain withers and dies because there is not enough moisture for its growth. A heavy rain, however, offers the prospect of enough growing time for the plant to flower and produce seeds. Unlike other desert plants, such as cactuses, these wild flowers have no special adaptations as mature plants that fit them for desert life. They are much like wild flowers anywhere. The secret of their success lies in their seeds. Slowly, after countless generations, the seeds of desert wild flowers have undergone a process of evolution called *natural selection*. In other words, they have been "selected" by their special adaptations to grow in deserts while other plants cannot.

As we might expect, larger desert plants, such as trees and shrubs, have made remarkable adaptations in their seeds too. For example, the seeds of ironwood, smoke tree, and palo-verde grow only in arroyos. These seeds are made in such a way that they will not germinate until their coatings are scarred by torrents of water rushing down the arroyo channel after a heavy rainstorm. In this way the seed is assured of enough moisture to establish itself as a new plant. Even more startling is the fact that the seeds of desert plants will not sprout unless the water comes from above. They are

Wild flowers carpet the Arizona desert after winter rains (left). Nine weeks later the blossoms have withered and died (right), but not before the plants have produced seeds for next year's crop. Many desert annuals bloom only in winter, others only in summer. Neither winter nor summer bloomers sprout unless there has been enough rainfall to supply the moisture they need to flower and produce seeds.

More than 5000 kinds of wild flowers grow in the deserts of North America. Perennials, such as the two lilies shown here, usually bloom after winter rains and grow long enough to store new supplies of food in underground bulbs or root stocks before they wither. The amount of moisture necessary to produce copious blooming of desert annuals is difficult to measure. However, truly spectacular wild-flower displays occur in spring if rainfall of more than one inch has accumulated in November and December.

The desert lily resembles the familiar Easter lily. Because of the flavor of its bulb, in Spanish it is called ajo, *meaning "garlic."*

The spotted gilia blooms only in March and April if an adequate amount of rain falls during the winter months. In a few weeks it produces seeds, then dies.

DESERT WILD FLOWERS

The desert five-spot grows in sandy soil in the Sonoran, Mojave, and Colorado Deserts. This four-inch annual blooms from February to June.

After favorable winter rains, the Mariposa lily often carpets acres of desert soil with blossoms that range in color from yellow to red, white to lavender.

The one-inch-high ground daisy produces flowers on each of its many branches. This perennial wild flower has a long taproot that works its way downward through the coarse soil of dry, rocky ridges.

SAND MAT

TURKISH RUGGING

ROCK GILIA

Some desert annual wild flowers are among the tiniest flowering land plants on earth. A few grow as high as three or four inches, while others never reach one inch. Because they are so small that you have to get down on your stomach to see them, they are called belly plants by botanists.

covered with a water-soluble substance that keeps them from germinating until it is removed by certain acids that are formed as the rain leaches downward through the soil. Water from below does not contain the acids that dissolve seed coatings.

Of course, even the hardiest desert plant loses most of its seeds anyway. Long before rain comes, many seeds are eaten by rodents, birds, or such insects as weevils. Wind-driven sand buries some seeds too deep to grow. Others may be blown great distances, ending up in habitats unfavorable to their successful growth, as would happen with a seed blown into a salt desert. As a consequence, only a small percentage of the seeds from a single plant will live to produce new plants, and this means that each plant must bear many more seeds than are needed for the survival of the species. In most cases this "overproduction" is high. Thousands of seeds must be released to produce one plant that will live to maturity.

The ability to grow and reproduce rapidly when rain comes has enabled many desert plants and animals to survive in their habitat. Roughly paraphrased, this is a "shape up or ship out" rule of evolution. If a species does not do well, it may soon be gone entirely.

This points to water as the main problem for life in the desert. The soil is fertile enough to support massive growths of at least some species of plants, and the sun furnishes an abundance, even a superabundance, of energy. What is lacking is water. But since at least a little water is absolutely essential to life, the plants cannot fight the drought—they have nothing to fight it with. All they can do is wait. The best waiters, so to speak, are the best evolutionary prospects.

Snow in the desert

Booming thunder and raging torrents are not the only signs of rain in the desert. Sometimes gentle rains fall for days, especially in winter, soaking the ground and turning large areas into muddy morasses. And sometimes the desert can be covered with moisture even when no rain has fallen for months. When you walk across the desert in early morning, your shoes may become wet with dew. The days may have been hot and dry for a long time, yet the plants are bathed in moisture, especially in summer.

86

Scientists have tried to measure this dew to determine how much there is. But dew is not so easy to measure. For one thing, it is constantly forming and evaporating, so that little ever accumulates in one place. For another, the moisture you find on leaves may be only partly dew; the rest may come from inside the plant, for all green plants exude a certain amount of water in the food-making process.

Nevertheless, dew does form whenever the earth and the objects on it cool to a point at which the vapor in the air condenses to water. You can see it happening on a summer day when the side of an ice-cold glass becomes beaded with moisture. By frequent testing of certain patches of land, researchers have been able to tell how much moisture is available to plants in a given period.

Several new ideas have resulted. First, dew is common even in many of the hottest deserts, and occurs on nearly half the nights of the year. Second, the hotter and drier the day, the more dew will form at night. This is because the hotter the land becomes during the day, the more rapidly this heat is reradiated back into the atmosphere at night— and it is reradiation that cools the land and the plants to the point at which dew will form.

If rapid reradiation occurred every night, the amount of dew formed annually might equal fifteen inches of rainfall. On some nights, however, reradiation is blocked by low clouds or haze or dust, in which case the land stays warm during the night and no dew forms. All things considered, dew probably accounts for a sizable amount of usable moisture each year in the Arizona desert. Precisely how much good this extra moisture does is a matter of disagreement among the specialists; but certainly it does no harm, and possibly it may account for the relatively rich vegetation in some otherwise arid regions. In addition, many small animals obtain a large percentage of their daily water intake from dew-wet plant leaves.

Beyond this, in the deserts of the United States, even the southernmost ones, snow is not unusual. On high deserts and those in northern areas, snow falls every winter, sometimes in great quantities. On southern deserts such as the Big Bend country of Texas and the saguaro deserts of Arizona, an inch or two of snow is likely to be recorded each winter. Snow has even fallen in the hottest of all American desert regions, Death Valley.

Snow in the desert, where it seems so out of place, is an-

Sheathlike yuccas, dusted with snow, weather out a storm in the Chihuahuan Desert in Big Bend National Park, Texas. Snow and low temperatures are not rare in the deserts of western North America. North of Big Bend at El Paso, a record low temperature of 5° below zero has been recorded.

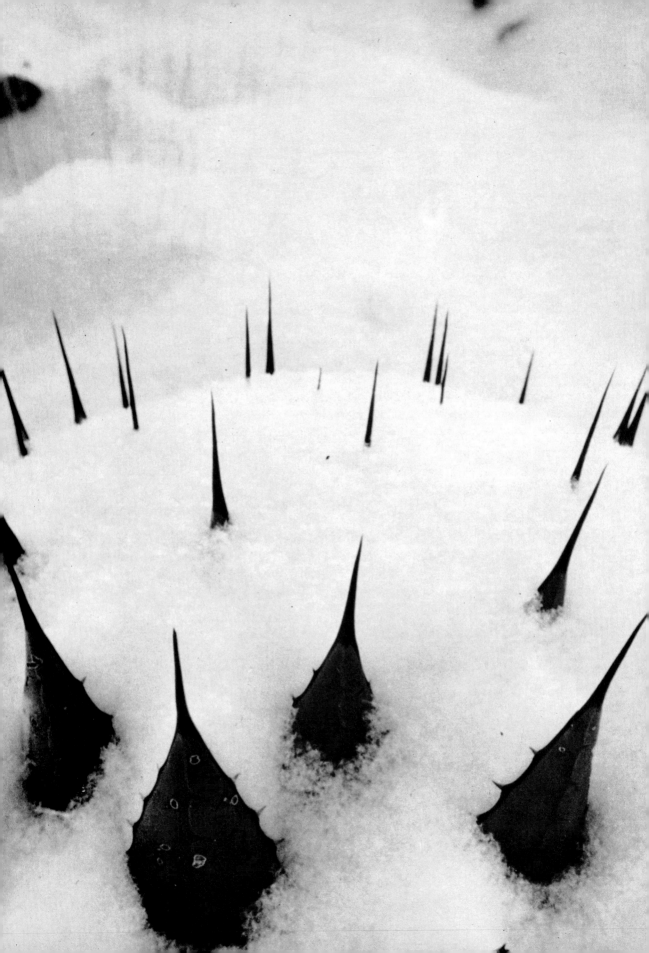

The spiny tips of a century plant thrust up through a blanket of snow. Unlike the water of summer cloudbursts, slow-melting snow, when it does fall in the desert, sinks deeply into the hard-packed soil.

other photographer's delight. Heaps of glistening snow on the deep red sandstones of Monument Valley, for instance, or on the granite rocks and yucca forests of Joshua Tree National Monument make dramatic pictures indeed, and at the same time explode the myth that deserts are always hot. Deserts can freeze—hard.

Pediments and playas

Scenery and more scenery is the desert's trademark. Sometimes towering snow-capped mountains loom above the desert floor. More often only the battered tops of old, worn-down mountains are visible, half-buried in the soil eroded from their own slopes. In the Great Basin Desert of Nevada one range after another was raised by upheavals in the earth millions of years ago, then reduced again by wind and water. Remaining today are the fantastic shapes of beautifully colored desert rocks.

Pediments are long, gentle slopes stretching from mountain slopes toward the desert floor. They are composed of layers of eroded material that are often more fertile than the salty soils of the desert floor below.

These centuries of erosion have filled the valleys between mountain ranges with sand and gravel. Long gentle slopes reach from either side toward the center, where they become the valley floor. These slopes are called *pediments* (after the Greek word for the low slanting roofline of temple architecture) and are probably the commonest feature of the American desert. They have been so long in forming, layer on layer, as eroded rock washed down from the mountains, that their soil is relatively fertile compared with the open wastes of the level desert.

Elsewhere erosion has created huge natural bridges, arches, mounds, knobs, shapes of every description. Most of this erosion has been the result of hundreds of thousands of years of wind. Flying grains of sand have been driven across the desert, each grain like a tiny chisel sculpting the rocks, smoothing them, cutting away the softer parts, until the desert has been turned into an immense gallery of natural abstract designs. To a certain extent water erosion has helped too, especially where rivers have cut through mountain rock to form deep canyons and bridges.

More than eighty arches attract visitors to Arches National Monument, Utah.

Many of the most striking rock formations are the remains of old volcanoes. These volcanoes originally consisted of a hard core, called a *volcanic plug*, surrounded by outer slopes of softer rock, lava, and ash. In time the softer parts wore away, leaving the core to stand alone, a stark pinnacle rising from the sand. Sometimes several such "chimneys" can be seen in one place, monuments of prehistoric time casting their shadows across the desert.

On maps of desert country you can see that some valleys have no outlets. These are natural basins, with all streams and rivers running toward the center. Many of these basins contained great inland lakes during the Ice Age. (The Great Salt Lake in Utah is but a remnant of a much larger lake called Lake Bonneville.) Today, however, most of these basins are dry, but in times of rain the water rushes down the dead-end streams and collects in the lowest part of the basin, forming a *playa* (the Spanish word for beach and temporary lake). This water is trapped; it has nowhere to go but up or down—up in the form of vapor or down as slow seepage into the earth. Because the desert does not readily absorb water, most of the water goes up. It evaporates, leaving a residue of salt picked up from the soil during the water's slow downward seepage.

In this way great salt flats are created. Seen from a mountain, they shine brilliantly in the distance, conspicuous features of the desert landscape.

Many salt flats have been intensively mined, first by Indians, then by white men. One of the largest exposed salt deposits in the United States is Searles Lake, California, where the upper layer alone is more than seventy feet thick. Older salt flats, millions of years old, have been buried underground by changes in patterns of erosion on the surface. In parts of New Mexico and western Texas, deep mine shafts have been sunk for the extraction of *potash*, a kind of salt used in the chemical and fertilizer industries. One of these hidden salt deposits extends for 200 square miles.

Somewhat similar salt deposits are found along low parts of the coast, as in southern Florida. There the ocean occasionally floods inland; the sea water covers the land, then slowly evaporates. Each time this happens, new layers of sea

A tabletop-flat playa cracks beneath the drying sun. After storms, run-off water from the mountains accumulates in this natural basin. Gradual evaporation and seepage of the water leave the playa paved with a layer of salt.

Once an active volcano, Shiprock rises 1400 feet above the desert in New Mexico. Erosion has worn away less resistant rocks, leaving only a hard volcanic neck. The tall needlelike spike in the foreground is a vertical vein of hardened lava.

93

The water in Lake Mono, California, is so saturated with mineral salts that great towers of travertine as much as twenty feet high grow from it, crystal by crystal.

salt are deposited. In some parts of the world men create salt deposits by pumping sea water into flat fields called *salterns* and then letting it evaporate in the sun.

In areas where the soil has been made saline, some desert plants often grow, for example, cactus, yucca, and *Salicornia*, a salt-tolerant shrub. The Cape Sable area of Everglades National Park at the southern tip of the Florida peninsula is one of the finest coastal "deserts" in the country. Another is the region of sand dunes on the North Carolina coast. In these coastal areas, however, it is the salt spray carried by wind passing over the ocean and shifting sand that creates desertlike conditions, not the aridity of the climate. Strictly speaking, they are not deserts according to our definition, nor are the many parts of the world that man himself has made barren through his wasteful practices. Nevertheless, it is worth noting that desertlike conditions exist in many isolated places; some of them have a good deal less plant and animal life than the deserts do.

The land dries out again

It has been some time since the rain ended. For several weeks the sky has been cloudless and bright. The arroyo is as dry as if it had never held so much as a trickle of water. Whatever water there was either has evaporated, has been used by plants and animals, has sunk into the earth, or has run off in streams and rivers.

For a while the nightly condensation of dew helps keep the desert fresh, but not for long. Drought takes hold again, flowers wither and die, the relative humidity decreases. Gradually, one by one, puddles and pools dry up, forcing the animals back into their water bondage.

Birds, mammals, reptiles—all gather at the water hole. If the water fails, life fails, or becomes dormant, at least for many species. Precisely this has happened many times in history, to men as well as other animals. Some species, such as the bighorn, or wild sheep, have been brought near extinction by a combination of overhunting, domestic animal

Lined up at a desert water hole, bighorn sheep await their turn for a drink. In times of drought, the big sheep sometimes use their curled horns to root out succulent bulbs. They also butt open barrel cactuses and feed on the juicy pulp inside.

disease, and loss of water holes to man, who converted the desert springs to his own use.

Directly or indirectly, all life depends on water. Where does that water come from?

Some, as we have seen, comes as rainfall, collecting on the surface in streams, pools, shallow wells, or other natural basins. But in many regions this surface water is insufficient for the animals and men who dwell there. Their water must come from deep in the ground.

An enormous reservoir of water lies underground in all regions of the world. It fills the cracks between deep rocks and saturates the layers of soil; it flows in underground rivers and collects in underground lakes. The upper level of this ground water is called the *water table*, and the precise depth of the water table in a particular area can be of the utmost importance.

In many regions the water table is at the surface, because the surface terrain dips below it. The result may be a spring,

a natural outpouring of water from a fissure in the ground. In some locations, usually along the base of a hill or a cut through the mountains, many springs may appear, showing that the surface of the land breaks across a water-bearing layer underground. Often springs are extremely good water sources, continuing to flow even when serious drought prevails on the surface; and since the water travels for long distances underground, filtered through sand and soil, it is likely to be pure. In the desert a spring is a godsend—it may be the major year-round source of water for thousands of members of the desert community.

In many places, however, the water table is so far below the surface that there are no springs; then only a deep well can tap the underground reservoir. Sometimes wells are drilled through solid rock to astonishing depths before they reach underground water, and sometimes, when a well is sunk in an unfortunate location, no usable water is found at all. Pumps are usually needed to raise the water from

Natural springs such as Quitobaquito in Organ Pipe Cactus National Monument, Arizona, support an entirely different kind of plant and animal life than do the dry desert slopes that surround them.

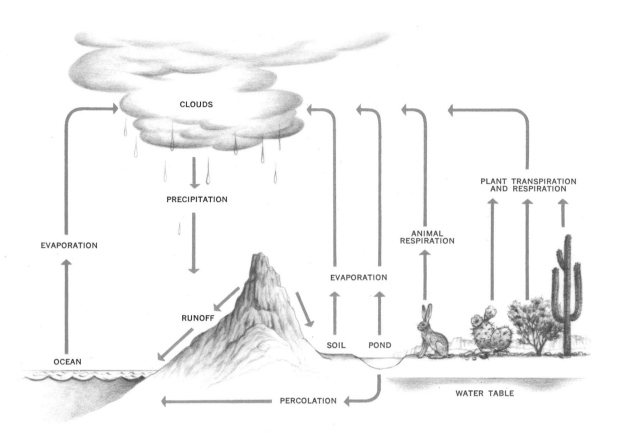

CLOUDS

PRECIPITATION

EVAPORATION

PLANT TRANSPIRATION
AND RESPIRATION

ANIMAL
RESPIRATION

EVAPORATION

RUNOFF

SOIL   POND

OCEAN

WATER TABLE

PERCOLATION

All plant and animal life depends on water. The ultimate source of all the earth's water is the ocean. When ocean water evaporates, the vapor condenses to form clouds. The precipitation (rain and snow) from the clouds falls back into the ocean or to the surface of the earth. Much of the water falling on land runs off in rivers and is returned to the sea. Some, however, sinks into the soil to replenish the water table, or is trapped in lakes and ponds. This water is used by plants and animals and then is returned to the atmosphere to become clouds again.

deep wells; but sometimes the water rises naturally, forced up by its own pressure, in which case the well is called an *artesian well.*

Whenever it rains, some rain water sinks into the earth or pours down natural crevices to replenish this great subsurface reservoir and keep the water table at its customary level. Under normal conditions the water table will not vary appreciably from year to year, especially since the water seeps for long distances through the earth, so that rain falling in one area may eventually replenish the water table in another area hundreds of miles away. But unfortunately conditions are not always normal. In recent years and in certain places, man has used the underground water faster than it has been replaced by natural processes, with the result that the water table has fallen far below its former levels. Springs vanish. Deeper wells must be drilled; more expensive pumping equipment must be used to bring the water to the surface. Trees die, fields turn brown, and grasses are replaced by cactuses and mesquite.

Worse yet, the lowering of the water table may leave air spaces underground. Layers of rock that formerly were supported by water pressure may collapse. Already the earth is subsiding beneath some desert cities where people have pumped too much water out of the earth. Buildings crack and pavements buckle. The need to conserve water is becoming increasingly evident—for more reasons than one.

Low water

As the desert dries up again, the water bondage of plants and animals is dramatically illustrated. If you go each day to a lookout point on a mountain where you can see across the desert floor, you will be able to watch the greenery turn brown before your eyes. You will see the meandering lines of green that mark the streams winding through the brown countryside: the green of cottonwoods, sycamores, hackberries, willows, and baccharis, or batamote, that grow along the banks.

Around a spring, a community of plants entirely different from the world of the flats may exist. Red or yellow monkey flowers sometimes grow in colorful masses. Brilliant yellow columbines may fringe the edge of a spring or stream. Delicate maidenhair ferns add a touch of elegance. You could

An irrigated cotton field stands out in vivid contrast to its parched surroundings. Yet in many areas the present blossoming of the desert presents a serious problem because water is being pumped from the soil faster than nature can replenish it.

call a place like this a *microhabitat*. This in fact is the term used by scientists to mean any self-sustaining small natural unit. It is a tiny world of moist, luxuriant growth within an immense desert. Of the many kinds of microhabitats, probably the easiest to study are those in canyons and valleys, where the steep slopes on either side cut off the rest of the world; but the microhabitat of a desert spring, far off in the remote wastes, may be even more important in terms of its life-giving and life-saving functions. It may be all that supports the animals from a large region of desert during the long drought between rains.

Extremes of dryness

Months pass without rain. Heat waves shimmer above the desert floor, and plants wither. Evening primroses, locoweed, datura, penstemon—all are affected. Now even the cactuses begin to shrivel. The thick pads of prickly pears shrink like dried figs and turn yellow or purple. The saguaros grow thinner; their accordion-pleated trunks contract in folds as their inner moisture is used up.

Some lizards and insects bury themselves in mud and stay there for months. Other insects—the powerful fliers such as dragonflies and wasps—may range far out over the desert, many miles from the region of their birth. As toads, lizards, and insects vanish, hard times set in for animals that depend on them for food. And as vegetation dies, the rodents that live on it grow leaner and scarcer. Then the coyote and hawk, the badger and owl come upon hard times too.

Of course nearly every region, practically speaking, experiences lack of moisture at one time or another. Even the rich greenery of New Jersey or Virginia can be badly damaged in summer if there is no rainfall for a few weeks. Farms and orchards may suffer great damage. Cities may be hit by acute water shortages.

On the fertile prairies of the Midwest prolonged droughts can change grasslands into "dust bowls." Usually other factors are operating as well: improper farming methods or overgrazing by cattle and sheep. But drought is what kills the grasses in the end. The dead plants blow away, then the loose soil turns to dust—so much dust that it blackens the sky—a "black blizzard" which can be far worse than anything in the desert.

The thorny pads of one species of prickly-pear cactus become purple in times of drought or cold weather. At other times the plant may have a light purple tinge or be completely green.

100

But the situation is critical only because the inhabitants of the prairies—human, animal, and vegetable—are not adapted to conditions of dryness. Desert drought is longer and more acute and occurs in regular cyclic fashion. If life in the desert goes on anyway, it is because that life has become adjusted to severe environments. Even though hot, dry winds parch the desert for weeks, and plants wither and die, their leaves crumbling into the soil, most somehow survive. Such flowers as sand verbenas and four-o'clocks bloom here and there, providing a touch of color that is all the more dramatic because it is the only color in sight.

The drought goes on

The longest drought on record in the United States was in Bagdad, California, in 1912–1914; there no rain fell for 760 days—two years and a month without water. One of the longest droughts in history occurred in a South African desert—the Kalahari—that went twenty-nine years without rain.

The plants and animals of the desert are hardy, it is true, but they have a limit of endurance. The giant saguaro, which may weigh fifteen tons and contain 80 per cent water, sometimes survives years of drought, but eventually dies if there is no rain. Lotus seeds found in a Manchurian peat bog were planted to see if they would grow; they did, even though they were dated by radiocarbon at 1250 years old! But it is not known how many desert seeds could keep alive that long.

In one sense a drought is abnormal: it is a period of less than normal rainfall in an area where "normal rainfall" is calculated partly on the basis of weather records and partly on the basis of vegetation, animal life, soil, and other observable factors. But in another sense droughts are perfectly normal features of the world's climate. They are part of global weather patterns that have existed for centuries. They have been commonplace throughout history, both human history (there is scarcely a year without a drought recorded somewhere) and geologic history as scientists reconstruct it from evidence in the earth's record.

Ancient sandstone cliffs reveal disarranged layers that were once the surfaces of sand dunes. Break open the sandstone along a hardened line and you may find a footprint—the fossilized track of a lizard that ventured out on the desert millions of years ago. We know that the ancient

The jumbled beds of De Chelly sandstone in Arizona are actually the dunes of a widespread desert that covered much of western North America in the Permian period, more than 230 million years ago.

101

The shallow, wide-spreading roots of the prickly-pear cactus soak up moisture even from rain that dampens just the soil surface.

The deep roots of mesquite frequently extend down sixty feet or more to tap the water table.

Sunken stomates help the century plant endure drought. Tiny openings on leaf surfaces are necessary for the intake of carbon dioxide and the release of oxygen during photosynthesis. Water also evaporates through stomates, but in the century plant and many others the stomates are placed in shallow pits that help cut down water evaporation by shielding the stomate from drying air currents.

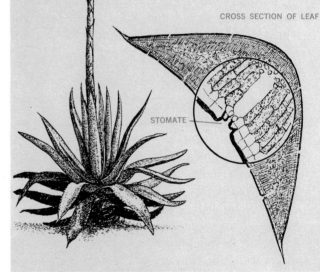

CROSS SECTION OF LEAF

STOMATE

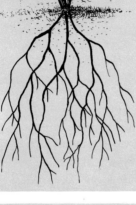

Succulence helps the barrel cactus resist drought. In dry weather the plant becomes shriveled as stored water becomes low.

In wet weather the barrel cactus grows plump as special storage cells fill up with water.

Leaf shedding helps the paloverde conserve water. When moisture is plentiful, tiny leaves manufacture food.

As soon as moisture becomes scarce, the leaves are shed to cut down on water loss, but photosynthesis continues in the chlorophyll-containing bark.

Root toxins produced by the roots of creosote bush reduce competition for water by killing plants that grow too close.

ROOT TOXINS

A waxy covering on creosote-bush leaves slows down water loss through the leaf surface. By reflecting heat, the shiny covering may also help to keep leaves cool.

RAINY SEASON

A compressed life cycle enables annuals such as the purplemat to evade drought. Germination occurs only when moisture is abundant enough to ensure the plant time to flower and produce seeds. Some annuals bloom only after winter rains, others after summer rains.

DRY SEASON

DESIGNED FOR DROUGHT

In the long evolutionary history of desert plants, the crucial factor of their survival has been water supply. Water on the desert is not only scarce, it is undependable. When rain falls, it often falls in torrents. Yet the storms may be followed by long periods with no precipitation at all. Strangely enough, many desert plants use water freely when it is plentiful. During the rainy season, some desert plants actually lose more water through transpiration than do plants living in areas of abundant rainfall. But with the onset of drought, water loss is radically curtailed. Desert plants have evolved a remarkable array of adaptations for surviving water shortages. Cactuses, for instance, resist drought by hoarding water when it is plentiful, then drawing on their reserve when it is scarce. Other plants, such as desert annuals, evade drought by remaining as dormant seeds during dry weather. Still others endure the effects of drought by shedding their leaves, thereby reducing water usage to a minimum. Whether the adaptation is in leaves, stems, or roots, or in a combination of these, whether the adaptation is shedding, rolling, shrinking, or some other, desert plants, on the whole, are perfectly fitted to an environment that offers an abundance of water one day and none the next.

deserts were extensive because their sandstone remains today cover tremendous areas. The Coconino sandstone of northern Arizona, for example, covers an estimated 32,000 square miles and in some places is 1000 feet thick.

The utter dryness of the period when the Coconino sandstone was formed, more than 230 million years ago, prevailed in other parts of the world as well. Geologists call that time the Permian period of earth history. There were probably more deserts at that time than at any other, except the present. Remains of Permian sand dunes and salt deposits have been found in Kansas, Texas, and parts of Europe.

Another time of widespread deserts was at the end of the Cretaceous period, about 63 million years ago. Earlier, life had been dominated for a long time by a large group of reptiles, the dinosaurs. Some were rather small and insignificant, but others were ninety feet long—the largest land animals ever known. They were well adapted to the humid conditions that prevailed during most of their time on earth;

Except for the Gila monster, the 8¼-inch plant-eating chuckwalla is North America's largest lizard. When annoyed, it threatens by opening its mouth. If this fails, it dashes into a rock crevice and puffs up its body more than half again its normal size. A predator will find it nearly impossible to dislodge the lizard from its place of refuge.

they lived in moist forests, swamps, and wet grasslands. At last drought came. Swamps dried up, and grasslands turned to desert. Temperatures fell, especially nighttime temperatures. Small fur-bearing animals, better adapted to the new conditions, increased rapidly in number, scurrying about and stealing eggs from dinosaur nests. Finally the great reptiles died out. Their miniature cousins, the lizards and snakes and turtles, survived in the new arid environment because evolution equipped them with adaptations that fit them for desert life.

Drought, then, is nothing new. It is part of the continuing process of the weather. There is a tendency for dry years to occur in groups, interspersed with groups of normal or even wet years. They have come and gone for millions of years.

Cycles of wet and dry

Rain comes again at last. Small white clouds appear over the mountains and rise swiftly into thunderheads. Lightning flashes, thunder rolls. The wind drives eddies of dust along the arroyo. The drama of the rain is re-enacted, and it will be followed, as usual, by the drama of the drought.

In times of moisture, the vegetation turns green, and seedlings sprout, flowers bloom, and cactuses grow full and round. Millions of rats and mice become healthier and beget other millions of rats and mice. The predators in turn grow fat and strong—the owls, coyotes, kit foxes, bobcats, and others. When the dry time comes, as it will eventually, the opposite will happen—the vegetation will wither, and animals will grow lean and hungry.

For generations and for ages the life of the desert, linked so closely to water, will wax and wane to the rhythm of the wet and the dry, one pulsation in the incalculable rhythm of the universe.

Against a mosaic of cracks, a single rabbit bush blossoms on a fast-drying mudflat. The rainy season in the desert brings about a striking change in the animal and plant life that flourishes there. It is a time for the reproduction of species and, for many, a time to gather the energy necessary for the dry days to follow.

107

Survival
in a Harsh Land

WEST OF the San Andres Mountains in southern New Mexico is a ninety-mile-long valley—ninety miles of rough, waterless desert. Nearly four centuries ago Spanish explorers in Old Mexico traveled northward through this valley to establish the first white settlements beyond the Rio Grande. Later their descendants, fleeing hostile Indians, retreated through the same valley, dropping in scores as death by thirst overcame them. They called their route *Jornada del Muerto*—Journey of the Dead.

Farther west, where the Colorado River empties into the Gulf of California, deserts stretch in either direction, a huge arid basin. The Spanish name for the region was *La Palma de la Mano de Dios*—the Palm of God's Hand. It was an appropriate name, signifying the landscape's awesome beauty and at the same time warning travelers who entered the desert that they placed themselves in the hands of God.

Not for centuries was the desert tamed. In 1849, when the Bennett–Arcane party left Salt Lake City for California, bound for the gold fields, they crossed desert after desert. Their supplies dwindled. Their water gave out. They came to occasional springs, but the water was so alkaline they could not drink it. They killed their oxen and drank the blood. Finally, in a broad valley they came to a halt, unable to continue. Several died. When at last they found a way across the mountains to the green land on the other side, the survivors looked back on the place of their torment. They called this desolate place Death Valley—and so it is called to this day.

Man and the desert

To keep cool when temperatures rise, all mammals must expend water. Man is no exception. On a hot day in the desert a man will lose great quantities of water through sweating. It has been estimated that a man of average weight walking for eight hours on the desert of southern California in July should drink three gallons of water to maintain his water balance.

When a man in the desert cannot replenish his body's water fast enough to make up the loss through sweating, his body will gradually lose its ability to keep cool. His temperature will begin to climb. The rate of climb will be slow at first, and the sufferer will merely feel light-headed and tired. He can still be saved if he finds water. But then suddenly the "explosion point" is reached. His temperature rises quickly. His tongue swells. His heart beats faintly, so that his blood circulates poorly, and his breathing fluctuates. Within a short time his temperature zooms to 107°–108°–109°. By then no amount of water can help him.

This doesn't mean that man cannot live in the desert. Many civilizations have flourished in the desert, in ancient times and in our own. But because the human body needs water, man must adjust in special ways to the conditions of the desert. Chiefly this means the use of special skills and techniques—what we call "cultural adaptations"—that may

Looking into the inferno of Death Valley, California, from a point appropriately called Dante's View, you can see spectacular alluvial fans and extensive salt flats. Death Valley was probably formed about eight million years ago. Its present appearance, however, is barely more than a million years old—only yesterday in geological time. If all the rocks, silts, sands, and other debris carried into Death Valley since it was formed were removed, the floor would be 10,000 feet below sea level! Today, after eight million years of erosion on the surrounding mountain slopes, it is only 282 feet below sea level. Even so, it is the lowest point in North America.

An Apache woman gathers prickly-pear fruits used to make jam. Desert Indian tribes, such as the Pima and Papago, Hopi and Navajo, have learned to utilize the plants and animals of their land for food, clothing, and shelter, as well as for household items as simple as brooms.

range from the immense water systems of some ancient and many modern nations to the almost uncanny desert lore of certain primitive peoples.

African Bushmen who live in the Kalahari Desert, for instance, can tell by looking at the surface of the ground whether there is water beneath it, even though the inexperienced traveler can see nothing to show that water is there. By inserting slender tubes into the sand, the Bushmen can suck up the hidden water—perhaps only a few drops at a time, but enough to sustain life.

If the members of the Bennett–Arcane party had been lucky enough to have a Bushman with them, they probably would have reached California safely. But their own knowledge fell far short of what they needed for their desert journey. Not only were they unable to find hidden water; they passed within sighting distance of several good springs they failed to recognize, springs that could have given them all the drinking water they needed.

The truth is that most desert springs are mere moist places

in the ground—seeps or sumps—where the vegetation is a bit greener than elsewhere. It takes a practiced eye to recognize them from a distance. This was just the kind of cultural adaptation that the early desert travelers lacked, although it was not long before some of them—prospectors, cowboys, scouts—began to learn the ways of desert survival.

Coping with thirst

Of all living creatures, man alone is capable of making a cultural adaptation. Other animals cannot; neither can plants. If they are to survive in the desert, they must make a physiological adaptation; their bodies must change to meet the conditions of life in a dry country. No single animal or plant can make such a change by itself; the process of physiological adaptation requires centuries of evolution.

Thus the desert is a barrier to the movement of many species. A bear, equipped by nature with a fur coat to withstand the cold of the northern forests, would be definitely out of place in a southern desert. A birch tree, accustomed to abundant moisture in the woods of New England, would wither and die if transplanted to the Arizona desertland. A trout from a mountain lake would probably not fare well if it were placed in a desert lake where the water might be salty and the water temperature above 90°.

Nevertheless there are many animals in the desert—even fish. They have made the necessary physiological adaptations. One unusual desert fish is the small pupfish less than an inch in length, a member of the Cyprinodont group. The entire known population of one species consists

The entire world's population of one species of pupfish lives in a small pool called Devil's Hole, near Death Valley. A few other species live in other parts of the desert. Holding on in lakes left over from the Ice Age, these interesting animals have become adapted to life in highly salty water.

of some three hundred fish in a spring called Devil's Hole at Ash Meadows, Nevada. So far as anyone knows, they have been there for thousands of years—the remnant of a much larger population from prehistoric lakes which covered the area. The lakes dried up, and the pupfish died out, except for this tiny community still hanging on in Devil's Hole. The pupfish can withstand greater salinity than most ocean species. Because this fish is a particularly interesting aspect of desert life and because its existence is so precarious, Devil's Hole was added to Death Valley National Monument in 1952—and a gravely endangered species is thus protected. A similar species of pupfish occurs in the pond and springs at Quitobaquito in Organ Pipe Cactus National Monument.

But what about camels? No other animal is so closely associated with the desert. Why shouldn't the camel thrive in the American Southwest? More than a hundred years ago Edward F. Beale, an enterprising Navy lieutenant, thought of this while he was crossing the desert from California to the East. He presented his idea to the government, and in 1855 Congress set aside $30,000 for the purchase and importation of camels. A shipment of sixty arrived the following year at Indianola, Texas, and Beale was assigned to lead them in a caravan to California.

It was a successful trip. And why not? Camels can carry loads of up to 1000 pounds and can go for ten days or more without water. They also can feed on bitter, tough desert plants. They seemed the ideal form of transportation for many desert operations.

But Beale's experiment was never carried to a successful conclusion. The first American camel riders, unaccustomed to the animal's rolling gait, got "seasick." Mules and horses stampeded whenever they saw or smelled a camel. With a little ingenuity these difficulties could have been overcome, but when the Civil War broke out Beale was called to other duties and his project abandoned. The camels were turned loose in the desert, where they roamed for a time; many an old-time prospector blinked incredulously when he saw a camel sauntering in the distance, as much at home as if it were in Arabia. Eventually, however, the camels were wiped out by settlers.

So camels failed in the United States. Ironically, they once lived naturally in this country, long before modern man. In fact, the camel family most likely originated in North Amer-

The fossil camel shown here flourished in the New World more than 13 million years ago during the Miocene epoch. Today a few small relatives of the camel, such as the llama, alpaca, and vicuña, live in South America, but the familiar camels of Africa and the Near East migrated to the Old World long ago.

ica. Fossil bones of ancient camels have been discovered from Florida to Alaska, and various species were common until about a million years ago. From North America they crossed to Asia over the land link that once existed between Alaska and Siberia, then spread to the Near East and Africa, where the modern camel gradually evolved. But the only species remaining in the Western Hemisphere today are the llama and guanaco of South America, where the llama especially is an important beast of burden; some varieties, such as the alpaca and vicuña, are raised for their wool.

Precisely why the original North American camels did not continue to flourish is a mystery. Perhaps competition from bison, pronghorns, mountain sheep, or other grazing animals was too great; perhaps the camels were killed off by such prehistoric enemies as desert wolves and lions; or perhaps some entirely different fate overtook them. We may never know.

Life without drinking

For whatever reason, camels could not survive in the North American desert. Other species could—and did. They had the necessary physiological adaptations. One of the most interesting of these is the kangaroo rat.

An 1857 painting records a moment of frustration for Edward F. Beale as his California-bound "Camel Express" leaves Fort Defiance, Arizona. After flourishing for a time, Beale's experiment with imported camels was abandoned, but not before the strange humped creature had played an important role in surveying wagon routes that later became highways.

115

You won't have much trouble seeing one on a desert trip. Chances are, if you scatter seeds or crumbs around your fire at night, a kangaroo rat will come bounding out of the darkness. It won't eat the food, but instead will stuff it into pouches in either cheek, as a chipmunk would, and carry it off to its den. Then the kangaroo rat will return for a second load, and a third and fourth, until the food is gone.

Each time this little creature enters or leaves your circle of firelight it will take a different direction, so you will have a difficult time tracking it to its burrow. But in the morning you will probably find a number of small holes in the ground beneath a sheltering bush or small tree. If you are patient, you may eventually see the kangaroo rat emerge from one of them, and you may even be able to watch it carry on some of its daily activities.

Except during the mating period, kangaroo rats live alone and jealously guard their underground stores of food. But sometimes one rat runs short, in which case it may try to "borrow" some seeds from a neighbor. The result is usually a vigorous set-to, with torn ears and gouged noses. Often at the height of the battle one rat will leap straight up into the air, two feet or more, to avoid its adversary. At other times, however, kangaroo rats play together harmoniously, "waltzing" on the sand or playing leapfrog. Sometimes two rats will scoot toward one another until their noses touch; then, as if someone had pressed a button, they will spring upward and backward, like mechanical toys.

Kangaroo rats are amusing creatures. They are also extremely important to the life of the desert, for they are a staple in the diets of many predators: snakes, hawks, owls, foxes, coyotes, bobcats, and badgers. If kangaroo rats were less numerous, these predators would be hard-pressed to make their livings. And if kangaroo rats were not so well adapted to the desert, they would not be so numerous.

You might think one of the kangaroo rat's adaptations would be the ability to withstand heat, but such is not the case. In tests, a group of rats was subjected to controlled temperatures. At 100° several rats died in less than three hours. At 105° most rats could last no longer than an hour and a half. Since the surface temperature of the desert often rises to as much as 160°, kangaroo rats could obviously not long endure in the open on an average desert day.

The solution to the problem is simple enough: the kangaroo rat merely stays in its burrow during the hottest part

One of the most perfectly adapted of all desert creatures, the kangaroo rat has evolved so remarkably to fit its arid environment that it no longer needs drinking water.

of the day. Other tests have shown that the temperature inside a kangaroo rat's burrow, even with a rat in it, seldom rises above 85°.

Fundamentally, however, the kangaroo rat's problem is not heat but dryness. Here too the kangaroo rat has adapted to desert conditions, but its safety device is far from simple.

Kangaroo rats often live many miles from water, as do the majority of all animals in the desert. However, they are not known to dig for water, nor do they eat the juicy plants that contain a high percentage of moisture. Their diet is chiefly dry seeds, small plant parts, and an occasional insect or lizard. Unlike many small animals, they do not drink the dew that forms on plants. Can they get along without any water at all? By no means. Every animal needs water because every animal loses some of its body fluids regularly. But the kangaroo rat has reduced this loss, over thousands of years, to such a low point that it can stay alive with very little intake of water—so little that the casual observer thinks there is none at all. And it is quite true that in the ordinary sense the kangaroo rat can remain alive without drinking.

In the first place, kangaroo rats lose little water through evaporation from the skin or breathing tracts. They do not sweat and they do not pant; they keep cool by avoiding the heat. In the second place, they have kidneys five times as powerful as those of men, and hence can produce urine so highly concentrated that the bodily wastes contain very little moisture.

In the third place, kangaroo rats lose much less water than many other animals in their feces, or droppings, which are produced in small black pellets, hard and dry. Finally, the kangaroo rat belongs to the rather large group of animals, including rabbits and shrews, that eat part of their droppings. Essential vitamins that have been produced by the fermentation of food materials in the lower digestive tract are obtained in this way. But at the same time, when this material is eaten, a certain amount of moisture that otherwise would be lost is reabsorbed.

By all these methods the kangaroo rat reduces its loss of body fluids and hence its need for fresh supplies of water. But it still needs some water. If it does not drink, where does the water come from? All animals produce a small amount of water within their own bodies when food is digested. The sugar in food is broken down, releasing not only carbon

The kangaroo rat spends the day in its burrow, where the temperature may be as much as 100° cooler than on the soil surface above. After dark this small rodent emerges from its underground home and bounds off across the desert in search of seeds and other plant foods.

117

Enraged by a neighbor's attempt to pilfer seeds from its underground granary, a kangaroo rat charges at the would-be thief, but the intruder leaps clear *(left)*. On a second try, the rats collide in midair; a wallop from the defender's powerful hind legs sends the marauder tumbling on its back *(right)*. By the time the scuffle ends, the loser may be badly scarred and battered. Yet on other occasions, these tiny hermits may meet in a less belligerent mood, seeming to enjoy a rousing game of leapfrog.

The grasshopper mouse gets most of its water by eating scorpions, insects, and other juicy prey. It seldom, if ever, needs to seek a drink elsewhere.

dioxide but hydrogen and oxygen, which combine to make *metabolic water*. The amount produced in this way is very slight; in most animals it has almost nothing to do with maintaining the balance of body fluids. But because the kangaroo rat has reduced its need for water so successfully, it can get along on the tiny amount of metabolic water created from its diet of dry seeds. Thus the kangaroo rat lives —as if by magic—without drinking.

Other animals do the same: the kangaroo rat is not unique in this respect. The common meal worm that lives in bone-dry bins of flour requires no outside source of water; neither do many animals that live in salt-water marshes where the water is useless for drinking, except for animals such as the sea gulls, which have special glands for excreting salt. In fact, if you include insects and birds, there are thousands of species that seldom or never take a drink: they are such efficient water users that they can live on the metabolic water alone.

Evolution has equipped the kangaroo rat in a remarkable way for its life in the desert. Many other kinds of animals, of course, live successfully in the desert too. They obtain water from water holes, from dew, from juicy plants, and from the bodies of animals they capture and eat. But few have the freedom of the kangaroo rat. It has escaped the water bondage almost completely, and so it can live nearly anywhere it chooses.

The cactuses

Just the opposite is true of desert plants. Each is confined to one spot, rooted for life. Plants can neither escape the heat of day nor move about in search of water. Thousands of different kinds of plants grow in the desert, but the ones everyone thinks of first are the cactuses. They are the desert plants *par excellence*. True, most of the more than 1600 recognized species are natives of the Western Hemisphere, but they now spread throughout the world, from Africa to the Far East, from the equator to the Yukon Territory in Canada.

They vary greatly in size and appearance, as might be expected. Some are immense: fifty or sixty feet high and weighing as much as fifteen tons. Others are tiny. Almost all have curious shapes, and many produce exquisite flowers. In general they share the same characteristics: they are *succulent*, or juicy; they have no leaves; they are spiny. These are the adaptations cactuses have made to the heat and dryness of the desert.

The cactus, which may contain a volume of 80 per cent water, is among the most succulent of plants. Some small cactuses are soft and fleshy and have watery tissues inside and a rubberlike covering outside. The larger cactuses need stronger structures to support their weight, and consequently they may be ribbed with woody tissues, much like an internal skeleton. When the cactus dies, the fleshy parts decay quickly, leaving the woody parts standing.

Because the cactus contains so much water, it can endure long periods of drought; when water is no longer available to the roots, it lives on the water it has stored inside, gradually shrinking as the water is used up. In time even the cactus will die if there is no rain. But it can survive long after most other plants have withered.

Partly this is because it lacks leaves. All plants exude moisture into the air from the surfaces of their green parts—they transpire. A full-grown oak tree, with thousands of leaves, loses a great deal of moisture through transpiration because

When a saguaro cactus dies, the fleshy outer part decays first, leaving only the tough inner ribs that support the plant's massive stems. Each indentation on a stem's fluted surface corresponds to a rib inside.

PRICKLY-PEAR CACTUS (SPINE)

HAWTHORN (THORN)

MOJAVE ROSE (PRICKLE)

Probably the most conspicuous feature of the cactuses is their spines, which are highly modified leaves. Thorns, however, are modified stems. The prickles on roses and other plants are neither leaves nor stems, but simply sharp outgrowths which may develop on any part of a plant.

Evolution has fitted the cactuses for life in regions of little rainfall by reducing their leaves to spines. In this way, the loss of water by evaporation through the thousands of tiny pores that cover leaves is curtailed. Food-making, which in most plants takes place in leaves, is carried on in the juicy green stems of cactuses.

all its leaves, taken together, amount to an enormous surface area. The cactus, by getting along without leaves, has a far smaller green surface, and consequently it loses far less moisture. The water contained inside the cactus lasts longer than that contained in the oak, quite aside from the fact that the cactus has proportionately more water to begin with.

In spite of its lack of leaves, however, the cactus carries on the same work of photosynthesis that other green plants do. It simply transfers the process from the leaves to the stems. A cactus, generally speaking, is green all over, which means that the chlorophyll—the green pigment associated with photosynthesis—is present in all the external above-ground parts.

The spines of the cactus serve several purposes. Obviously they help protect the plant from plant-eating animals, although some rodents, especially desert wood rats, and a good many insects are able to avoid the spines and reach the plant's fleshy parts. The spines also cast shadows; not very big shadows, but a cactus that is covered with tens of thousands of spines may get a good deal of shade. The spines break up the sun's rays and help keep the plant from getting too hot. The dense spines on some cactuses help diminish the air currents that pass over the surface of the plant, thus reducing loss of moisture from evaporation. At the same time, however, this results in a reduction of the plant's ability to lose heat to the surrounding air. Just what adjustments the cactus has evolved to compensate for this reduction in heat exchange is not clearly understood. It is thought that probably the spines help to maintain the delicate balance between heat exchange and the loss of water.

Cactus versus rodent

In a test near Tucson, Arizona, experimenters once planted 1600 young saguaro cactuses, half of them in the open and the other half in protective cages. Young saguaros are particularly appetizing to wood rats and other rodents. Within

A white-winged dove probes the depths of a saguaro
blossom for nectar. While feeding, the dove spreads
pollen from one blossom to another, thereby aiding
in the pollination of the cactus. Later, the dove
and other birds will feed on the ripened fruits and
distribute undigested saguaro seeds in their droppings.

two years rodents had killed 1470 of the young plants; they reached those in cages simply by tunneling under the wire. Other conditions caused the death of an additional 100 plants, so only 30 of the original 1600 survived.

In view of all this, how is it that the desert is so full of saguaros? It is because there are so many saguaro seedlings. A certain number are bound to escape the notice of foraging rats and mice, especially if they are growing in crevices or under protecting bushes and trees. The saguaro requires shade during the early years of its growth. Only young saguaros that take root beneath bushes or tall grasses ("nurse plants") will survive anyway, even if rodents do not eat them. It is fortunate, therefore, that the saguaro fruit is liked by birds, for birds are an essential link in the plant's propagation. When the sweet-tasting saguaro fruit ripens in June, it is eaten by birds, especially white-winged doves and Williamson's sapsuckers. The fruit is digested, but the seeds pass unharmed through the digestive tracts of the birds and drop to the ground beneath the trees in which the birds roost. There they remain protected and shaded until the next rain comes. Then they sprout, but even so, only a few survive to become mature saguaros.

The Tucson experiment might indicate that the spines of the cactus have little value as a protection against plant-eating animals. True, many saguaros and other cactuses are destroyed by rats and mice. But many others are not. Even those that are badly gnawed often survive to an old age, riddled with holes, nests, and tunnels. The cactuses persist in spite of all the eating and digging.

Evolution is a process that has gone on for millions of years. While the cactuses developed protective devices, plant-eating animals slowly perfected their foraging techniques, and the balance of nature was maintained. The spines of cactuses do not provide 100 per cent protection against plant-eating animals, but even the cleverest rodents cannot completely destroy the cactuses.

The many kinds of cactuses

Although there are larger species in Latin America, in the southwestern United States the saguaro is king of cactuses. Who could miss it? Fifty feet tall, ten tons or more in

Most saguaros are killed by wood rats and other rodents that feed upon them, but a few escape notice under protective "nurse plants" such as this paloverde. It is estimated that only 1 out of 250,000 saguaro cactuses becomes a mature plant.

weight, it branches capriciously—a striking silhouette on the desert landscape. In some places saguaro forests cover broad areas, with as many as sixty mature plants to an acre. And what you see aboveground is less than half the plant: a network of shallow roots spreads thirty-five feet in all directions. Strong, dense roots are required to keep the giant plant upright in high winds and to gather as much water as possible when the sparse rains come.

Saguaros do not grow in every dry region. In the colder deserts, where sagebrush and saltbush are common, the saguaro dies out. But the wonder is that it survives anywhere. Weevil larvae, rats, and mice feed on the seedlings. Bacteria spread from one saguaro to another by means of moths and other insects. The fruit of the saguaro is eaten by human beings, animals, and insects. It is estimated that only one of every 275,000 saguaro seeds produces a mature plant. After ten years the slow-growing saguaro is still only four inches high, and it takes more than a hundred years to reach maturity. Then the plant may live to a ripe old age of 250 years.

But the saguaro is only one of many interesting members

of the cactus family. On a single drive or hike through desert country, you may see an astonishing variety: the bristling cholla, which is a favorite nesting place for wrens; the organ-pipe, staghorn, hedgehog, pincushion, rainbow, claret-cup—the names are delightfully descriptive. The night-blooming cereus, with its twiggy stems and immense underground roots, is celebrated the world over for its extraordinary fragrance. Barrel cactuses stand plump and juicy, their scarlet flowers looking as if they had been stuck on with pins. Barrel cactuses provide food for many animals and birds, and the plant itself, still moist when many other desert plants have withered, is an important source of water for both animals and occasional desert travelers.

Cactuses grow everywhere

Cactuses are not limited to the desert alone. The cactuses are particularly well adapted to dry country, and hence their greatest development has occurred in the deserts of North and South America. But you can find cactuses growing natu-

The saguaro is the largest of all North American cactuses, some plants reaching heights of more than 50 feet and weighing more than 10 tons. They begin their growth in the shade of another plant, growing very slowly at first: it takes 25 years for the plant to reach a height of 2 feet. At 50 years the saguaro is 6 feet high. The first arms develop when the plant is 75 years old. Most saguaros reach a height of 35 feet by the time they are a hundred years of age. Some very old specimens have had as many as 50 arms.

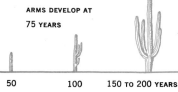

ARMS DEVELOP AT
75 YEARS

50   100   150 TO 200 YEARS

THE FLOWERING CACTUSES

Among the most beautiful of all desert flowers are those produced by the cactuses. The blossoms of these plants range in color from creamy white to the brilliant yellow of Engelmann's prickly pear *(left)*. Others are purple, magenta, pink, red, and orange. Some have a single blossom at a time, others may have many. The pincushion cactus *(top right)* has a ring of flowers that remain open for several days. It blooms twice a year, usually in April and again in July and August. The golden rainbow cactus *(bottom right),* for its size, produces among the largest of all cactus flowers. Whatever their color, shape, or size, the flowers of cactuses bloom from February to September, some for a single night, others for several days. They often supply the only color in the desert during the driest months.

The claret-cup cactus sends up a single flower stock topped by a large crimson blossom that dwarfs the tiny plant that produces it.

PRICKLY-PEAR CACTUS

BARREL CACTUS

JUMPING CHOLLA CACTUS

Cactuses vary greatly in form. Some are tiny plants only an inch or so high, while others tower thirty-five feet or more above the desert floor. Each species has its own arrangement of spines, in twos or threes, in starlike clusters, or in long straight rows. Some have pads, others are plump and round, and a few are treelike. Of the nearly 1000 kinds of cactuses known, more than half grow in Mexico and the southwestern United States.

rally from the Straits of Magellan to the far Canadian North. They grow in the jungle, on islands, and at the seashore. They grow in the Andes Mountains at elevations of more than 12,000 feet. You can even find them in the dry, rocky areas or sandy wastes of North Carolina, or in Mississippi, Massachusetts, Illinois, Missouri—practically anywhere.

And if you travel around the world, you will find that cactuses grow in extraordinary variety. In different habitats they assume many different forms. Apparently the cactuses produce new species quite easily, for you can find intermediate areas where hybrid cactuses appear—combining the features of two or three different species.

In other words, the evolution of cactuses is still going on. It has been a long process. No one knows where or exactly when it began, though there is good evidence that cactuses originated in tropical America. The earliest cactuses probably resembled other plants. Then they gradually lost their leaves, became succulent, and developed spines and intricate roots. Some grew smaller, turning into the miniature globular "pincushions" many people grow in tiny flowerpots; others grew larger, assuming treelike or vinelike form.

Man's hindrance

As it happens, the saguaro cactus offers us not only a splendid desert plant but a good example of what happens when human enterprise upsets the balance of nature.

The area around Tucson, Arizona, was acquired by the United States from Mexico in 1853, as part of the Gadsden Purchase. During the Civil War and for some years after, it remained a desolate region, the domain of Indians and prospectors. But in the 1870s it suddenly became the scene of intense activity in the Southwest's expanding cattle industry.

Much of the region was covered by tough desert grasses as well as by cactuses, mesquite, and other desert shrubs. The grasses were good forage for cattle, and in a vast get-rich-quick scheme cattlemen brought hundreds of thousands of cattle into the area. By 1890 the region already showed signs of overgrazing, and from 1891 to 1893 it suffered a severe drought.

The drought alone would not have done permanent damage to the desert vegetation. But because the grasses had been eaten off in many places, the soil became badly eroded within a few years, much of it carried away in newly formed gullies or arroyos. This heightened the effect of the drought. The result was an increase in certain types of cactuses, such as cholla and prickly pear, that could grow in barren soil, and a parallel increase in the wood rats associated with these plants.

But the saguaro, which had been the dominant cactus of the area, began to die out. It could no longer reproduce itself, for two primary reasons. First, tall grasses had formerly served as the "nurse" plants that shaded saguaro seedlings; with the grasses gone, the seedlings, exposed to direct sun, withered and died. Second, the increase in wood rats added to the destruction of saguaro seedlings, since wood rats are particularly fond of young saguaros. And the increase in wood rats was furthered by the vigorous campaigns of the cattlemen to eradicate the coyote, the rat's chief enemy.

The effects of overgrazing in Arizona are boldly evident today. In some areas, where grazing has been controlled, the saguaros have made a partial comeback. In others, especially in the valleys, the balance of nature was so seriously upset that it may never be the same again.

Hereford cattle forage in a degraded saguaro forest. Overgrazing has seriously decreased the numbers of saguaros; where great forests of these cactuses once stood, now low scrubby vegetation and prickly-pear cactuses grow.

*The mourning dove builds
a flimsy platform of twigs high up
in the thorny branches of cholla
cactuses. Its nest is so loosely
fashioned that you can see right
through it.*

SPINY HOMES FOR DESERT BIRDS

Many species of desert birds have overcome the shortage of
nesting places by making their homes in spine-studded cholla
cactuses. The thorns, in fact, may be of value in protecting
fledglings from snakes and other predators. Not only chollas but
other cactuses as well are used. Many species of birds, such as
owls, hawks, and woodpeckers, live in nest cavities or in the
branches of saguaros and organ-pipe cactuses. Were it not for
these large treelike plants some species of desert birds might
have no nesting sites at all.

*The female Costa's hummingbird
uses spider webs to lash her
compact cup in place.*

*The cactus wren throws together
a sloppy melon-sized ball of
grasses and twigs that has a tunnel
leading to its feather-lined interior.
Often when the wren moves out,
a white-footed mouse moves in.*

The yellow-blossomed paloverde grows only in dry washes where there is water a few feet underground. Mesquite, another desert shrub *(foreground)*, is not so restricted. It can send down roots as much as a hundred feet to tap subsurface water.

Equipped for survival

Cactuses are not the only plants well adapted to heat and dryness. The desert is a marvelous garden of other species as well. The ocotillo, for example, is a cluster of thorny stalks that looks like a bundle of fishing rods. In the spring it bears scarlet flowers on the tips. Unlike the cactus, the ocotillo has leaves; but when the drought comes, the leaves fall off, only to grow again when it rains. Another plant with the same ability to shed leaves in a dry period is the creosote bush, which gets its name from the smell of its leaves. When drought comes, most of its leaves fall off; so do twigs and whole branches; the bush looks dead. But small leaves and buds are hidden within the thicket of branches, and when rain comes, the bush leafs out and produces yellow blossoms. In fact, the creosote bush is one of the hardiest and most familiar of desert plants, ranging over millions of acres.

Many desert plants get along with few leaves, or with leaves that can be shed when necessary. Paloverde, beautiful smoke trees, and crucifix thorns all share this ability. By

The ocotillo, fringed with leaves and crimson blossoms *(left)*, blooms during the rainy season. Later, when moisture is at a minimum, blossoms have withered and leaves have been shed. Nevertheless photosynthesis continues in the green bark of the seemingly dead plant.

In spring, deep-blue blossoms line the thorny branches of the smoke tree, but with the onset of the dry season, its nearly leafless blue-gray twigs look like billows of smoke. This desert shrub grows in dry washes and depends on flash floods for germination. The tough smoke-tree seeds sprout only after rocks and gravel carried by floodwaters scar their coats. Only those seeds that have been carried 150 feet or more from the parent smoke tree germinate, because seeds carried shorter distances have not been sufficiently damaged. However, a seed carried more than 300 feet has been so severely injured that it dies.

the shedding of leaves, the loss of internal moisture through transpiration is greatly reduced. Since the plants must carry on photosynthesis in order to live, this function is transferred from leaves to stems, where the cells are able to manufacture sugars. The twigs of the paloverde, for instance, are covered with green bark.

Nothing approaching a complete discussion of desert plants could be contained in anything less than a very big book. There are literally thousands of plants: the yuccas, Joshua trees, elephant trees, and many more.

But all desert plants, by one means or another, have overcome the dryness of their habitat. Their unusual adaptations are what makes them so interesting. Mesquite can send down a taproot as far as sixty feet to reach moisture. The creosote bush exudes from its root-tips a substance that prevents other plants from growing around it, thus assuring it an adequate supply of moisture in a particular location. (Because of this, creosote bush sometimes is spaced perfectly regularly, as if planted by man.) Some of these plants have so many peculiar adaptive features that whole books have been written about a single species.

Whatever adjustments these plants have made to their environment, the fundamental principle is the same—adapt or die. In a thirsty land this means three things: get water; conserve water; as far as possible do without water. One way or another, this is what the desert plants and animals have done.

The strange elephant tree, or bursera, grows on rocky slopes in Organ Pipe Cactus National Monument, Arizona. If the bark of the short tapering trunk is damaged, it exudes a blood-red sap from the inner layers.

Ears for the hunter

When we think of the desert, we think of thirst; yet thirst is not the only problem of desert dwellers. Water alone will not support life. A large part of animal life in the desert is governed by hunger and the quest for food; and since the desert is a distinctive habitat, this quest requires special adaptations not found elsewhere.

When you are walking in the desert on a moonlit night, you may find (if you are lucky) that you have been joined by a half-seen shape that slips in and out of the shadows, now behind you, now in front. It moves so quickly that you see only a silvery, soft blur. Chances are, if you shine your flashlight on it, you will discover that your new friend is the little kit fox.

About the size of a large house cat, weighing about three and a half pounds, the kit fox resembles its distant cousin, the gray fox, in having a thick coat and a bushy tail. But its coat is buff yellow or grayish, with scattered black-tipped hairs: a perfect camouflage in desert moonlight. Although the kit fox ranges over nearly the whole western desert from Idaho to central Mexico, it is seldom seen, and almost never in daylight. Yet you will get a fading glimpse of a kit fox often enough if you spend much time on the desert at night, and you will find its dainty tracks in the sand.

Kit foxes are unafraid and rather curious about human beings, and yet shy; they are so quick and agile on their feet that another name for them is "desert swift." They live underground, in burrows that may extend eight feet before reaching the nesting chamber. There the kit fox spends the hot part of the day, and there once a year the young—called kittens—are born, four or five in a litter.

The kit fox preys on any small animals it can find, but its favorite is the kangaroo rat—to such an extent that the

The kit fox usually lives in flat open terrain, where it feeds on insects, kangaroo rats, and even scorpions. Its large ears are lined with thick hair that helps keep out sand when it burrows.

kangaroo rat has been called the "staff of life" for the kit fox. Often in sandy areas you will find rat burrows that have been dug open by foxes, although the fox is quite capable of stalking its prey on the surface. Wood rats, pocket mice, small birds, lizards, and insects are eaten too—even scorpions.

Most night predators in northern forests rely heavily on their sense of smell in searching for food, which isn't surprising when you consider that smells "travel" well in the humid air of the forestland. But the opposite happens in the desert. Smells vanish quickly in the dry winds. Whether or not kit foxes actually have a poor sense of smell is not known for certain, although there is at least one case on record where kit foxes passed within ten feet of heavily scented food without finding it.

But if the kit fox lacks a keen sense of smell, it makes up for it with an acute sense of hearing. A kit fox's ears are a good deal larger in proportion to its size than the ears of other foxes; they are broad and well pointed. Moreover, they can be moved independently, so that the kit fox can listen in two directions at once. At the slightest sound its ears twitch, listening for the direction and identity of its prey. Then this little mammal turns toward the sound, moving swiftly on its short, sturdy legs.

The desert at night is a continual murmur of small, dry sounds, most of them too slight for humans to notice—the rustle of a gecko crossing the sand, the rattle of a mouse among mesquite twigs. To hear these sounds at a distance, to recognize them and sort them out is a great advantage in the struggle against hunger. The kit fox's big ears are a helpful adaptation to life in the desert.

Even though the scorpion packs a wallop in its stinger-armed tail, many desert animals, including the kit fox, feed upon it. The painful sting of most American scorpions is not fatal to man.

Ears for the hunted

Nature does not distribute favors one-sidedly, however. If big ears are good for the predator, why not for the prey? No animal has bigger ears, proportionately, than the jack rabbit.

The huge ears of the black-tailed jack rabbit detect the presence of meat-eating predators and probably also help to regulate its body temperature. The delicate blood vessels lie so near the surface of its ears that excess body heat is thought to be radiated to the air through them.

140

You can't miss jack rabbits, especially in the sagebrush and saltbush flats that are their favorite habitat. Drive along the highway and you will see them bounding away in great leaps toward the bushes. Walk along a desert trail and you will scare them up easily, sometimes a dozen or more at once. Crouch beside an open area at twilight and you will see them feeding on leaves and grasses.

The jack rabbit isn't a rabbit at all, but a hare—the most common being the black-tailed jack rabbit. You will find it throughout the Great Basin and Mojave Deserts and into California, in fact throughout most of the West. In more southern areas, especially southern Arizona and New Mexico, you will see the larger antelope jack rabbit, which gets its name by flashing its white underside when running, like a pronghorn, which is sometimes called "antelope."

Because they are extremely secretive, not so much is known about jack rabbits as you might think. Most people never see them doing anything but running away. It takes time and patience to observe them in their ordinary routine.

The jack rabbit's home, or *form*, is a small hollow in the grasses made by bending grass stalks. Here it spends the hot part of the day. Here the young are born, already furred,

The black-tailed jack rabbit is extremely abundant in the desert. Chiefly nocturnal in its habits, it spends the night feeding on desert plants.

with their eyes open, and able to hop about. Soon they can take care of themselves. Usually the area inhabited by jack rabbits is criss-crossed by trails, or *runs,* and the hares can run and dodge among these pathways with great speed.

But doubtless the jack rabbit's chief distinction is its long ears. The antelope jack rabbit's ears may reach a length of eight inches or more. They are thin, delicate structures through which sunlight passes so easily that you can see pink blood vessels. Like the kit fox, the jack rabbit can move its ears independently, and constantly does. While feeding or resting, it twitches its ears continually in all directions, alert for the slightest sound of an approaching enemy.

Its enemies are many. Snakes, birds, coyotes, bobcats—and of course man. A rattlesnake will strike a jack rabbit with lightning quickness. Gopher snakes seize jack rabbits, especially young ones, and kill them by constriction. Coyotes can run down jack rabbits, at least if they catch them in the open. Bobcats spring on them from ambush. Eagles and hawks can strike suddenly from the air, dropping perhaps a thousand feet and snatching the animal with their sharp talons. Owls may pounce soundlessly at night.

With so many animals intent on making a meal of jack rabbits, you might think the population would be in constant danger of extinction. Not at all: it has remained stable. Partly this is because the jack rabbit reproduces easily and plentifully, like other species of hares and rabbits. Moreover, the jack rabbit also succeeds as often as not in eluding its enemies. Many are caught, but many get away.

Jack rabbits' ears and powerful hind legs are what saves them. With their ears they detect the approaching enemy before it can strike. With their powerful legs they leap and dodge to the nearest thicket. Once safe in a thicket—the thornier the better—they can rest secure from most of their enemies. Thus big ears are an essential part of the jack rabbit's adaptations to a perilous environment.

Color camouflage

Many other adaptations help desert animals hunt their food or escape their enemies. Coloration is one. The light-colored coat of the kit fox helps it sneak up on a kangaroo rat because the color blends almost perfectly with the moonlit desert. The antelope hare, by "flashing" its white underparts

Gopher snakes often prey upon young jack rabbits. This constricting reptile seizes its prey by the head and then throws ever-tightening coils around its body. The squeezed victim is then easily swallowed.

as it runs—first on one side, then on the other—sets up a broken pattern of color that tends to blur its outline and confuse its pursuer. Almost every animal has a color that bears some significant relationship to the habitat in which it lives.

No place to see this could be better than White Sands National Monument in New Mexico, a fabulous white desert near Alamogordo. The desert is not ordinary quartz sand, but grains of gypsum—white as snow, blown into fantastic dunes and billows. It is a strange, sterile-looking world. Yet life thrives there too. Yucca plants grow on the dunes, sending down deep roots to the moisture beneath. When the wind blows the gypsum away, the plants are left perched on pedestals, held in place by their roots.

Mice also thrive on the white sand dunes, but only because they are white mice: not the kind used in laboratories —these are pocket mice, miniature cousins of the kangaroo rat, common in many desert regions. Long ago they strayed out onto the gypsum desert and took up residence there. In time many of the darker-colored mice, easily seen against the light background, were caught by hawks and other predators, while the lighter-colored mice, harder to see

Flecked with black and white, a grasshopper is almost invisible against the mottled granite sand on which it lives. Other insects, spiders, and lizards in the Colorado desert are similarly camouflaged.

against the white gypsum, escaped. Gradually a light-colored form of pocket mouse evolved.

A few miles away from the white dunes is a black lava flow where a volcano once erupted. Pocket mice live on this black rock too; but they are dark-colored. And in the hills beyond, where the soil is reddish, the pocket mice are somewhat red in color. Within a small area these pocket mice have evolved in three different ways, and in each case they are colored protectively: they are inconspicuous against the background in which they live.

Some animals are so well protected by coloration that even in photographs you can scarcely see them. When you see a picture of a horned lizard on a laboratory table, you may think you would never be able to miss it, but in a picture of a lizard against its normal background of coarse sand and pebbles you can hardly see the reptile's outline. The variegated color patterns make it almost invisible. The long-tailed brush lizard, which spends much of its time in creosote-bush branches, looks so much like a branch itself that nine times out of ten you will not see it until it moves.

The insect-eating wolf spider generally is grayish brown, but on the granite sand in the Colorado desert it is light and slightly mottled—like the grasshopper *(opposite page)* from the same area.

145

These two horned lizards are camouflaged to suit their backgrounds. The lizard at the left lives in an area where the ground color is predominantly gray, while the lizard at the right inhabits a region of red soil. Horned lizards carry protective coloration a step further than the grasshopper and the wolf spider on the preceding two pages. When a horned lizard moves from a shaded area to a sunny area, its color becomes lighter. Of course, the lizard has no conscious control over this; the color change occurs when differences in heat and light set off an automatic rearrangement of the pigment granules in its skin. Even so, this adaptation benefits the color-changing lizard: although it spends much of its time on open sand in full view of would-be predators, it continues to flourish.

Adapt or die

The many adaptations to desert life that you can see in the deserts of North America would be hard to describe completely. In fact, since the animals and plants are what they are because of the adaptations they have made, a catalogue of adaptations would be almost the same as a complete description of the whole natural world.

Many kinds of adaptations have not been mentioned here, or have been only hinted at. The forms of behavioral adaptation, for instance: When the kangaroo rat dives into its burrow to escape the desert heat, this isn't something the kangaroo rat "thinks about" or "understands"; it isn't even a habit, as we use the term to describe human behavior. It is a completely instinctive and totally automatic pattern of behavior stimulated by the length of shadows, air temperature, and other factors that we do not yet know about.

Yet such behavioral adaptations are quite as much a part of evolution as are physiological adaptations. The kangaroo rat's instinctive escape into its burrow has taken as much time to develop as has its long tail or powerful hind legs. And it has just as much to do with the kangaroo rat's ability to survive in the desert.

Evolution is a long-term process, as we have seen. It takes millions of years to produce an entirely new type of animal or plant. Yet small changes may occur much faster than we realize. In fact, the interrelationships of plants and animals to each other and to their environment are constantly changing. It is a pageant going on before our eyes—if only we take the time to look.

Nearly indistinguishable from the pebbles that surround it, a living-stone cactus is an outstanding example of the limitless variety of adaptations evolved by desert plants in response to their environment. This plant is so well camouflaged that it usually is not seen by animals that might find moisture and nourishment in its succulent aboveground parts.

The Face
of the Desert

WHEREVER YOU GO in the desert regions of western North America, whether it be the Mojave Desert, the Chihuahuan Desert, or the northern Great Basin Desert, there are some things common to deserts as a whole: There is an obvious lack of available water, there are often soaring temperatures, the plants are sparsely distributed in the hard-packed sandy soil, and here and there are vast tracts of barren salt flats or rocky outcroppings where very little grows.

But even though a desert is easily recognized, the differences from one region to the next far outweigh the likenesses. In the desert, as everywhere else, the plants and animals live in definite groups called *communities*. In the Great Basin Desert, for example, there are two major communities. The northern Great Basin Desert is the land of sagebrush, the jack rabbit, and the cottontail, while the southern Great Basin Desert has a distinct community of shadscale and Ord's kangaroo rats.

Of course this does not mean that sagebrush does not grow in the southern Great Basin Desert, nor that Ord's kangaroo rat does not live in the northern Great Basin Desert. What it does mean is that certain plants and animals are more numerous, or *dominant*, in one area than in another.

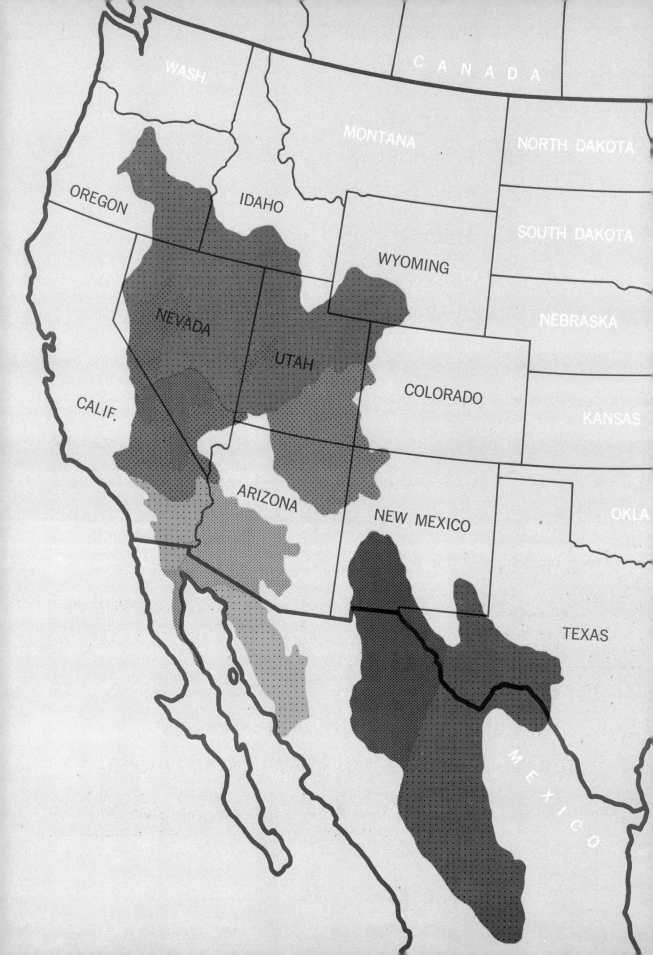

DESERT COMMUNITIES OF THE UNITED STATES AND NORTHERN MEXICO

GREAT BASIN DESERT

    Shadscale—kangaroo rat community

    Sagebrush—rabbit community

MOHAVE DESERT

    Creosote bush—desert kangaroo rat community

    Yucca—ladder-backed woodpecker community

PAINTED DESERT COMMUNITY
(PIÑON, JUNIPER, SAGEBRUSH, AND YUCCA)

COLORADO DESERT

    Kangaroo rat—creosote bush—saltbush community

    Ironwood—ocotillo—elephant tree community

ARIZONA–SONORAN DESERT

    Tall cactus—gila woodpecker—ocotillo community

    Ironwood—paloverde—mesquite community

CHIHUAHUAN DESERT

    Creosote bush—desert cottontail—yucca community

    Succulent desert community

There are several reasons for this, such as differences in annual rainfall, soil, altitude, temperature, and food.

Within communities, smaller units called *associations* exist. Along a stream bed in the Chihuahuan Desert, cottonwoods and willows replace saguaro cactuses, ocotillo, and paloverde. In this stream-bed association a population of animals thrives that is different from those that live in a drier association only a hundred yards away.

Thus each desert region offers the visitor an endless variety of plants and animals and, at the same time, displays living things that have adapted to deserts everywhere.

North to the mountains

Although quite different from the western deserts, southern New Mexico and western Texas are regions of marvelous beauty for desert travelers. Near the border of these two states lies Carlsbad Caverns National Park, New Mexico, visited by thousands of tourists. Those who fail to notice the rich desertland in surrounding areas are missing some of the most characteristic landscapes of the American Southwest.

Broad, flat valleys are covered with mesquite and creosote

bush, a panorama of vastness and solitude. Along the rocky foothills of the Guadalupe Mountains are rich growths of many impressive desert plants, including mesquite, cat-claws, sotol, and thousands of barrel, hedgehog, pincushion, and prickly-pear cactuses. A fine desert garden at Carlsbad Caverns National Park offers the visitor a good opportunity to identify the different species.

Returning to the Alamogordo area of New Mexico you find one of the most dramatic contrasts in all American desertlands. Head southward through the valley of white sand and black lava—an intense desert of extreme heat and dryness. On the western side are the Sacramento Mountains, where Sierra Blanca rises 12,003 feet—the southernmost alpine peak of the Rocky Mountains. If you take the highway leading up to Cloudcroft, New Mexico, you first enter the foothills, with fine growths of desert plants such as ocotillo and many cactuses. Next comes an extensive juniper and piñon pine forest, still extremely arid, with cactuses and crucifix thorns mixed among the conifers.

Above this is a belt of *chaparral*, containing desert scrub oaks, and then the zone of great ponderosa pines—tall, straight trees. Finally the forest culminates in a zone of spruces and firs, with groves of beautiful quaking aspens

Carlsbad Caverns National Park, located in the rugged Guadalupe Mountains of New Mexico, not only contains the largest caverns in the world but also has a wide variety of desert plants and animals. A large cactus garden is maintained for visitors to the park.

interspersed with meadows of lupines, penstemons, Indian paintbrushes, and other flowers. Here you will find plants and animals from northern regions, south of their usual ranges. From Cloudcroft you can look out and see the white sands far below, framed by the mountain forests. And if you continue upward—now it is a rugged climb—you will pass above tree line and emerge on the top of Sierra Blanca, where snow may linger much of the year.

Journeys up and down

Your journey from a hot to a cold climate is dramatic because it is compressed in a short space and time. It is a vertical journey—up the mountain—rather than an overland trip to a distant region. But you are not the only traveler.

Many others use this mountain too—especially birds. Some species that elsewhere migrate north and south save themselves the long journey by simply migrating up and down; they nest in spring in the high forests, then spend the winter

Two males and a female Gambel's quail search for insects and seeds in the rocky soil of the Arizona desert. Efforts have been made to reduce the hunting of these plumed game birds.

in the foothills or on the desert floor. White-crowned sparrows and other songbirds follow this practice, as do some larger birds, for instance the harlequin quail with its intent-looking expression, or the more ornate Gambel's quail with its bright markings and delicate head plume.

Perhaps the most spectacular bird you can see on the mountain is Merriam's wild turkey, which has a beautiful white or pale-buff barred tail, although you must be lucky to find it. Originally at least five kinds of wild turkeys were abundant throughout North America, but hunting has reduced their numbers in many places.

Another mountain migrant, one of the most attractive to tourists, is the mule deer, which in some places is so tame that it will eat out of the hands of strangers. The mule deer is a good deal stockier than the familiar white-tailed deer of more temperate environments, and the bucks have somewhat larger antlers. Its large ears give it its name. The local species in the Chihuahuan Desert is called Crook's mule deer.

Mule deer are not primarily desert animals, although they live in most desert regions. At one time they were common throughout almost the entire western part of the country.

An able flier despite its size, Merriam's wild turkey spends the day hunting seeds and insects on the ground. At night it roosts in trees.

157

The mule deer's large ears, resembling those of a donkey, distinguish it from the white-tailed deer. Living throughout most of the North American desert, a subspecies called Crook's mule deer feeds on such seemingly inedible plants as yuccas.

They are tough and adaptable, and can live well on a surprisingly unattractive diet, which accounts for their ability to survive in the desert. Normally they eat the twigs and leaves of bushes and low-growing trees, but they also favor cactus fruit and sometimes cactus stems. They can browse successfully on spiny yucca plants and Joshua trees. So long as they get enough to eat, they need very little water.

Like other deer, mule deer retreat to deep thickets in spring when the young are born and remain there during the summer while the fawns are growing. You may find them—or more likely their tracks and droppings—high in the spruce-fir zone of the mountains. But when autumn comes and snow creeps farther and farther down the mountainside, the deer migrate to the foothills or the desert floor.

The mule deer has few enemies. Coyotes take the sickly or aged, thus helping to keep the herds strong. In earlier times mountain lions, or cougars, undoubtedly preyed frequently on deer, but now the mountain lions are less common. A notable exception is at Big Bend National Park, where these interesting cats are quite common. Here, as

158

elsewhere where they exist, mountain lions do prey on deer and javelina, helping to keep their numbers in balance with available forage. Bobcats occasionally kill young deer by leaping on their backs and biting their necks and throats.

One way to get along in the wilderness, as we have seen, is through specialization; many highly specialized plants and animals flourish within the limits of their particular habitats. But there is also an opposite way—versatility, or a capacity for living in many habitats. In some areas, where the climate is changeable or the conditions of life are unstable, the plants and animals that can take advantage of different habitats may have a better chance to survive than those that are overspecialized. The mule deer shows a good example of the success a versatile animal has.

Seldom-seen desert cats

Jaguars originally roamed the deserts of New Mexico, Arizona, and southern California, living on deer, mountain

Weighing as much as 290 pounds, the jaguar is the largest cat in North America. These cats are now rare north of the Mexican border, but in former times they were probably abundant north of the Rio Grande, where they fed on mule deer, peccaries, turtles, and fish.

BIG BEND NATIONAL PARK

The rugged Chisos Mountains rise 8000 feet above rolling desert landscape at Big Bend National Park, Texas. The park, sixth largest in the National Park System, straddles the Texas–Mexico border where the Rio Grande carves a U–shaped bend through deep canyons. Much of the Big Bend country is semiarid highland plains dotted here and there with yuccas, prickly-pear cactuses, and other Chihuahuan Desert plants, including sotols, agaves, and forests of Spanish daggers.

sheep, wild pigs, and smaller game. But when the ranchers came, establishing their herds of cattle and horses, the jaguar soon developed a taste for domestic animals, with the result that a war of extermination was launched against the beautiful big cat. Nor was it only because of the safety of horses and cattle; men feared jaguars and told hair-raising tales of encounters with them. Most of these stories were exaggerrated, although it is true that the jaguar is occasionally known to attack human beings without provocation.

Today the jaguar is seldom seen in the United States, but it is a sight worth looking for. Up to eight feet in length, weighing as much as 250 pounds, the jaguar is a graceful, powerful animal with a beautifully marked coat. Normally the jaguar attacks its prey by springing upon it and dragging it to the ground, but this cat can be a formidable runner when the occasion requires, pursuing its quarry along the ground, into trees, even into water. Crouching, leaping, running, climbing—its movements are as quick and agile as a house cat's, in spite of its size.

One reason jaguars used to live along the southern border of the United States is the presence there of the only wild pig native to North America, the javelina, or peccary. This is primarily a Mexican species, but fair numbers of javelina live along ravines and dry washes in the bush-covered desert ranges. They are tough little animals, without much resemblance to their fat domestic cousins. But they have a distinctly piglike snout with which they can root out lizards or insects from the rocky soil.

Covered with salt-and-pepper-colored bristles, the javelina has a compact body and a big head, small nimble feet, and extremely sharp teeth, which make it a difficult catch for anything but a swift-running jaguar or mountain lion.

Young javelina make good pets, and in Mexico are often tamed. You may see one trotting behind a group of children in many a small Mexican market place. But when they get older, javelina turn wild again and can be extremely ferocious. Cowboys once thought it a great feat to rope a wild javelina, but many paid dearly for their sport when their horses' legs were gashed by the victim's teeth.

Like other tough desert animals, the javelina survives through its ability to eat almost anything—spiny cactuses, roots, tubers, lizards, snakes, whatever it can find. All of these things are nourishment for the javelina's apparently indestructible digestive system, and the cactuses give it the

Peccaries, the only pigs native to the New World, usually travel in small bands. These shy animals eat mostly plant foods, though they occasionally feed on small animals that they root out of the ground.

moisture needed during periods of drought. Javelina spend the hot hours of the day resting beneath thickets or in hollow places, then come out in evening to roam in bands of a dozen or so, searching for food.

In a sense, neither wild cats nor wild pigs are true desert animals. They are more closely associated with tropical or subtropical forests, and have not made the striking adaptations to heat and dryness that characterize many native desert dwellers. Still, both cats and pigs do live in the desert. They are versatile animals; they can find a means of survival almost anywhere. This is also true of many other species.

Like the jaguar, the ocelot is essentially a cat of the Latin American jungles, but occasionally lives in the United States along the southernmost desert ranges, particularly in thicketed areas and remote canyons. The ocelot is much smaller than the jaguar—three and a half to four feet long including the tail, about thirty-five pounds in weight—but beautifully marked and graceful in movement. Adult ocelots will fight furiously if attacked, but they never bother human beings if undisturbed. Young ocelots can be tamed easily if they are caught when still kittens, and they make fine pets.

The ocelot, smallest of North American cats, is still occasionally seen along remote stretches of the Mexican border. These cats live in desert thickets and mountain areas, where they feed on small mammals and birds.

163

The Painted Desert

Northwestward from the Chihuahuan Desert you will find the Painted Desert, land of brilliant colors and surprising shapes—one of the most popular areas in the Southwest for vacationing visitors.

Flat, broad, dry, and surrounded by low mountains, this is the land of the mesas—flat-topped "islands" rising above the desert floor, some huge, some small. The cliffs and canyon walls of ancient sandstone are banded with hues of red, orange, yellow, and brown. To the west is the Grand Canyon, and to the northeast are the remote peaks of the central Rockies.

The immense Navajo and Hopi Indian reservations are the main attraction of the area for many visitors, and rightly so. The Hopi, with their great communal dwellings built like fortresses atop mesas, and the Navajos, with their extensive sheep-grazing operations and nomadic communities, are both well known today for their mastery of such Indian crafts as weaving, metalworking, and painting.

It is high country, most of it above 3500 feet, which means that the winters can be cold and often snowy. But the summers are hot, with intense thunderstorms, high clouds, and brilliantly clear atmosphere. At night there are often beautiful displays of sheet lightning along the horizon. The desert floor is barren sand or windswept rock in many places, and in other places it is covered with low scrub—yucca, sagebrush, and a variety of grasses.

At the southeastern end of the desert is Petrified Forest National Park, containing six separate areas in which fossilized tree trunks 150 million years old can be seen. Logs from ancient forests at one time were apparently washed into swampy basins and covered with volcanic ash. Gradually they became saturated with mineral deposits of quartz, extremely hard and brightly colored, with the result that today they form a spectacular display for visitors.

To the north is Canyon de Chelly National Monument, cut by deep canyons of red sandstone; still farther northward is Monument Valley, where thousands of photogra-

A colorful cross section of a petrified log reveals that every cell of the once living tree has been replaced by silica and other minerals dissolved in water. The replacement is often so perfect that scientists can study the cellular structure of these ancient trees by looking at microscopically thin slices.

Streaked with rainbow hues, the colorfully banded sandstones and sediments of the Painted Desert stretch for miles in northern Arizona, southern Utah, and western Colorado and New Mexico.

phers have lingered with delight. Other natural attractions of the region are Rainbow Bridge, Sunset Crater, Meteor Crater, Coal Canyon, and the Wupatki ruins.

Animal life in the Painted Desert, as in most deserts, is dominated by rodents and reptiles. Mice, ground squirrels, prairie dogs, gophers, and rabbits are common. Many lizards inhabit the region, and a few snakes—including the desert rattlesnake, its colors ranging from pink to reddish-brown, a subspecies of the common western rattlesnake which lives in all western states.

Rattlesnakes are common throughout the desert. At least twelve species inhabit the western deserts of North America, the largest and most dangerous being the diamondback rattlesnake. The diamondback may be as long as six feet, even seven in rare instances. It is bold and, unlike other rattlesnakes, will hold its ground when provoked. This, coupled with the quantity and strength of its venom, makes it especially dangerous, though no rattlesnake can be considered "safe."

One of the most interesting and characteristic rattlesnakes of the West is the sidewinder, a powerful snake about two feet long. It can be recognized by small projections over its eyes that look like horns. The sidewinder gets its name from its manner of crawling, going diagonally in a series of wriggles. This leaves a peculiar track in the sand, consisting of separate J-shaped marks, almost as if the snake had jumped from one mark to the next. The tracks are common in the sandy desert and easy to follow.

Desert rattlesnakes are most active at night and in summer, like other desert snakes. Except in very warm regions, they hibernate underground in winter. If you want to find a sidewinder, you will probably get one by driving along a dark-paved highway on a summer night and keeping a lookout for snakes on the road surface. Wise desert campers do not place their sleeping bags on the ground in summer, and they do not walk in the desert at night without a strong flashlight and good shoes. Even so, it is sometimes impossible to avoid stepping on a rattlesnake, especially since they are marked and colored to blend with their surroundings. Stepping on a rattlesnake does not necessarily mean you will be bitten, but you may be. It is a good idea to carry a snakebite kit, which you can get at most hospitals, doctors' offices, or drugstores.

Rattlesnakes belong to the pit viper family, which also

Erosion is slowly uncovering these two fossil tree trunks at Petrified Forest National Park. Many other trees of this ancient Arizona forest, which flourished 160 to 170 million years ago, lie buried under as much as 300 feet of sediments.

CANYON DE CHELLY NATIONAL MONUMENT

A reminder of men who long ago lived in harmony with the desert, the ruins of a prehistoric Indian dwelling perch at the lip of a cave in a sheer sandstone cliff. White House Ruin is one of many ruins in Canyon de Chelly National Monument, Arizona. Archeologists suspect that a prolonged drought in the Painted Desert led to their abandonment in the thirteenth century. The man near the circular opening of a ceremonial chamber, or kiva, at the foot of the cliff appears dwarfed by canyon walls hundreds of feet high. Today Navajo Indians live along the bottom of the canyon where they grow peaches and raise sheep.

Coiled at the base of an agave,
a diamondback rattlesnake
avoids the direct rays of the
desert sun. Like many other
desert animals, this rattler has
a pale color and indistinct
markings.

includes copperheads, moccasins, and the fer-de-lance. The
name comes from an extraordinary adaptation shared by all
these snakes—little pits between the eyes and nostrils. These
pits are really organs for detecting heat, so sensitive that
they amount to a sixth sense. A rattlesnake, for instance,
can detect the presence of another animal at a considerable
distance just by the heat the animal's body radiates into the
air. The heat-sensitive pits in the snake's head pick up these
radiations, and the snake can follow them until it finds its
prey. Then the rattlesnake strikes, injecting its venom, and
immediately lets go. The victim dies very quickly, where-
upon the rattlesnake devours it at leisure.

In addition to the rattlesnakes, one other highly venomous snake lives in the western deserts. The Sonoran coral
snake, related to the more familiar coral snake of Florida, is

beautifully marked with bands of red, yellow, and black and is slender and about two feet long. It is seldom seen, since it is active exclusively after dark. It has the ability to flatten its body in such a way that it can fit into extremely small rock crevices or into small underground passages during the day. Presumably the venom of the Sonoran coral snake, like that of other coral snakes, is highly dangerous to man, but there has never been a published report of anyone being bitten by one. The Sonoran coral snake feeds on other snakes and lizards.

Rattlesnakes and coral snakes are not the only snakes that inhabit desertlands. By far the greatest number of desert reptiles are harmless creatures that serve as important members of desert food chains. They feed on a variety of small animals, including insects, frogs, rodents, and young birds. In turn they are eaten by road runners, owls, hawks, and numerous mammals.

The pronghorn

Snakes and other small creatures are only a few of the wild inhabitants of the Painted Desert. Maybe you will see a herd of pronghorns. The pronghorn is often called an antelope in the United States, but it is not a true antelope.

Not long ago—perhaps two hundred years—there were

The sidewinder spends the day half buried in the sand, usually in the shade of a rock or bush. The hornlike projections over each of its eyes are thought to prevent sand from interfering with its vision.

*Especially fond of brushy areas,
the agile whip snake moves along
as rapidly through the branches
of low shrubs as it does
on the ground.*

*Named for the peculiar scale
at the tip of its snout, the yard-long
mountain patch-nosed snake lives
at higher elevations in many
desert areas.*

HARMLESS DESERT SNAKES

A surprising variety of snakes thrive in the American desert, though they are not nearly so numerous as some people imagine. A few are poisonous, but the great majority of these colorful reptiles are harmless creatures that play an important role in desert food chains. They feed on insects, small rodents, and birds. Hawks, road runners, badgers, skunks, and other animals in turn prey on them.

The common garter snake lives in the Great Basin, Painted, and Chihuahuan Deserts, wherever there is a permanent source of water.

Seldom more than eighteen inches long, the spotted night snake hunts after dark. Though harmless to man, its slightly poisonous saliva probably helps to subdue lizards and other small prey.

A leftover from the Ice Age, the pronghorn is an exclusively North American mammal that never spread to other continents. Not related to the Old World antelopes, these interesting cud-chewers belong to a group that once had many more members. Under strict government protection, their seriously reduced numbers have now been increased to a point where some hunting is allowed.

millions of pronghorns in western North America from Saskatchewan to Mexico. Until about twenty years ago, the pronghorn population was decreasing to a dangerous degree because of hunting and the reduction of their grazing land. But in another sense the pronghorn has been its own worst enemy. Intensely curious, pronghorns will often walk toward a hunter instead of running away.

Smaller than most deer, the pronghorn is usually about three feet high at the shoulder and weighs about 125 pounds. A mature buck can run faster than forty miles per hour. Graceful, fleet-footed, they are beautiful animals with buff-colored coats trimmed in white on the rump and underneath. Their faces are marked with black and white, and their horns curve backward and inward, making elegant headdresses.

Pronghorns have extremely keen eyesight and can spot

an intruder at a great distance. When danger arises, they come from all directions, joining in a single file with a mature doe at the head and a buck, the master of the herd, at the rear. Then they flee. At the first sign of danger, they "flash" their white rump patches; special skin muscles raise the white hairs, making them visible from a distance.

Serious efforts to conserve the remaining pronghorns have been made by state and federal agencies and by such private organizations as the Boone and Crockett Club and the National Audubon Society. Herds have been established at the Charles Sheldon Antelope Refuge in Nevada and the Hart Mountain National Antelope Refuge in Oregon; animals from these herds have been sent to other public and private refuges throughout the western United States and Canada. In addition, wild pronghorns still exist in widely scattered areas.

The horns of the pronghorn are hollow outgrowths of the skin of a small bony knob, or pedicle, which is exposed when the horn is shed. Unlike the horns of bison and sheep, they are grown anew each year. If horns are present in the females, they are smaller than those of the males and are not branched.

Monument Valley, on the Arizona–Utah border, is one of the most spectacular areas of the Painted Desert. Unscalable cliffs of Navajo sandstone rise hundreds of feet above the desert floor and cast thirty-five- to forty-mile shadows late in the afternoon. The Navajo sandstone was formed during the Jurassic period, more than 135 million years ago, and consists of evenly sized sand particles that were once sand dunes. This rock formation varies in color from gray to red and can be seen not only in Monument Valley, but also in Zion Canyon, Glen Canyon, and Natural Bridges National Monument.

Where there is suitable land for the pronghorn, however, the herds have increased to such an extent that hunting on a managed basis can now be conducted without danger of reducing the herds to extinction. The combined population of pronghorns in Wyoming, Montana, South Dakota, North Dakota, and Colorado is estimated to be about 150,000. Other sizable herds are increasing under state management in the Great Basin and in Arizona, Nevada, New Mexico, and Texas.

But the possibility of building up a pronghorn herd on a scale large enough to suggest the original numbers of these magnificent animals is no longer feasible because the wide expanse of grazing land that would be needed is now used to support cattle and other livestock.

The Great Basin—a cold desert

The cold, arid lands of the Arctic tundra in many ways resemble the hot deserts of western North America. Because of scant rainfall, the adaptations of the plants that grow here are remarkably similar to those of plants in hot, dry climates.

Northward again, you cross into the Great Basin Desert, the largest American desert. It must be stated clearly that there is a real difference between hot deserts that occasionally become cold and true cold deserts. *Hot deserts* are those of subtropical latitudes or low elevations; the Sonoran, Chihuahuan, and Yuman Deserts and the desert of Baja California are examples. There the sun burns fiercely much of the year and snowfall is rare.

The sagebrush-covered flatlands of the Great Basin Desert stretch out for hundreds of miles below mountain peaks such as Nevada's 13,063-feet-high Mount Wheeler.

But *cold deserts* are just as much deserts as are hot deserts, and the term is not the contradiction it seems at first. Remember that what makes a desert is lack of moisture, not a particular temperature. Oregon has cold deserts. So do California, Utah, Nevada, and other states. They also exist in Asia, New Zealand, and Africa. Cold deserts are too high or too far north to be as consistently hot as other deserts, hence they retain more moisture and have fewer sweltering days. But they are still arid in comparison with the land around them, and they are accurately called deserts.

The farther north you go, the more desertland you will find. The great treeless barrens of the Arctic are usually not termed deserts, but that is what they are. The annual precipitation on the Queen Elizabeth Archipelago, far north of continental Canada, is about six inches. Enormous areas are nothing but stony wastes with sparse grass and occasional tiny flowers. Some arctic plants grow in the compact form that also characterizes hot-desert plants, an adaptation that in both cases reduces transpiration and saves water.

So it is clear that the kind of plant and animal community you will find anywhere depends to a large extent on the nature of the climate. If the climate is cold, we expect more fur-bearing animals and fewer reptiles. If it is moist, there will be a thicker cover of vegetation, which will support a larger number of plant-eating animals. Many other factors likewise exert an influence: prevailing winds, existence of neighboring seas or mountains, number of days of sunshine. All these factors are interrelated. Any natural community—in the desert or elsewhere—is an immensely complicated system of connections and dependencies, and what we know about nature is still far less than what we do not know.

Of course there are very few fixed boundaries to deserts. You won't find a signpost that reads PAINTED DESERT on one side and GREAT BASIN DESERT on the other. To a certain extent, desert scientists disagree not only about the size of deserts but even about their names. Nevertheless, the general boundaries of the Great Basin Desert are well known: they enclose nearly all of Nevada and Utah, parts of Wyoming, Idaho, and Oregon, a corner of Colorado, and a snippet of California.

Such a vast desert cannot be described easily. The main distinction between the Great Basin and other deserts that

Unlike the ocean-loving brown pelicans, white pelicans are fresh-water birds. They nest by the tens of thousands on inland lakes in western North America. Huge nesting colonies are found on remote islands in Utah's Great Salt Lake. Since this lake is too salty to support fish life, these resourceful birds commute as much as a hundred miles to fresh-water lakes, where they gorge themselves, and then return to feed their young.

lie to the south is the typical vegetation. Not many cactuses grow in the Great Basin, nor much creosote bush; it is a region of sagebrush, saltbush, and greasewood.

Generally speaking, the Great Basin is high, with elevations from 2000 feet to as much as 6000 feet above sea level. It is flat, consisting of huge valleys and plateaus divided by mountain ranges. In some areas sagebrush and greasewood grow densely for miles and miles, like a vast sea; in others the ground is bare and rocky. There are salt deserts in Utah; in Nevada, north of Winnemucca, there is a region of spectacular sand dunes averaging seventy-five feet in height. In Oregon there are views of beautifully colored bluffs, with mesas and buttes rising from the desert floor.

The soil throughout much of the area is salty, and so is the water. Utah's Great Salt Lake is only one of many saline bodies of water. At one time, hundreds of thousands of years ago, much of the desert was under water; huge salt lakes stretched for thousands of miles between mountain ranges. Today geologists can show you bands of waveworn rocks high on the mountainsides where the water level used to be. Often they find important fossil remains of prehistoric men and animals along the ancient shores of these vanished lakes.

But salt is not the only mineral deposit of the Great Basin. Gold, silver, copper, lead, uranium, and other metals are mined throughout the region from Colorado on one side to California on the other. In the old days prospectors accom-

A hungry young pelican all but disappears into its parent's enormous pouched bill to feed on a fishy soup that the adult bird makes in its stomach.

panied only by a burro wandered across the desert in search of ore deposits, sometimes for years without a find. Today geologists and mining engineers work in the same regions, armed with complex electronic tools for determining what lies beneath the ground.

Many wild animals of the Great Basin are the same as those you have seen in other deserts—coyotes, jack rabbits, hawks and owls and vultures, rattlesnakes, lizards. But a few are especially associated with sagebrush country, and one of the most interesting is the sage grouse. Like its eastern cousin, the ruffed grouse, this bird makes a fast getaway when flushed from cover, and consequently is considered good sport by hunters. But in winter, when it has been feeding almost entirely on sagebrush leaves, its flesh is bitter-tasting and "sagy."

The sage grouse is more colorfully marked than the eastern grouse and has yellowish-green wattles. Like all members of the grouse family, it is characterized by remarkable behavior during the courtship period in spring. The male grouse make little clearings throughout sagebrush and prairie country, and each spring they flock to these clearings by hundreds. The clearings are called "strutting grounds," and there the male grouse put on their "display," each competing with the others to attract as many hens as possible.

During its display, the male puffs up as big as he can, spreads his tail into a sharp-pointed star, arches his wings, and blows up the bright-colored air sacs on his breast and at the sides of his neck. Then the male struts, beating his wings and walking stiff-legged. When fifty or a hundred males all put on their displays at the same time, it is about as comical a performance as you are likely to find in the world of nature.

But not to the sage-grouse hens. They are attracted, or perhaps overawed. In any event the male that makes the biggest show claims the prize. And not just one hen; perhaps half a dozen—a whole harem!

A male sage grouse fans out its tail in full display as it begins its strut, or courtship dance, which may win it a harem of hens. The instinct to return to the same breeding grounds each year is so strong that when a road was put through one of these areas, the grouse courted in the center of it.

182

After a few preliminaries such as spreading its tail, advancing three or four steps, and gulping two quick breaths of air, a male sage grouse begins to fill its lungs and the air sacs on its breast (left). Three inhalations and exhalations in rapid succession fill the sacs to capacity (middle). Then the grouse raises its wings, thereby contracting the muscles surrounding the air sacs. As the air is released, the bare spots on the grouse's breast disappear (right), and there is a loud "plop," audible half a mile or more on a quiet morning.

COURTSHIP RITUAL IN THE GREAT BASIN DESERT

During the winter, sage grouse live in flocks that may number in the hundreds. They feed on sagebrush leaves and live in apparent peace with one another. But with the approach of spring their behavior changes. Males begin to congregate in breeding areas, and after several weeks of fighting they are divided on the basis of their strength and aggressiveness into categories, from a superior master male and his chief rival to guards and outsiders. The master of the flock mates with as many as 80 per cent of the hens, his chief rival with 13 per cent, and less aggressive males with a few other females. After mating, the males break up into small groups and spend the summer in remote areas. Later in the fall they band together and are joined by the hens and young birds in the winter feeding grounds.

A sage-grouse hen seems uninterested in the elaborate display of a strutting male. After each strut the male pauses to observe its effect, if any, on a female.

Mountain lions and bobcats

Both bobcats and mountain lions range throughout the Great Basin as well as other deserts, although their numbers have been greatly reduced. Because of this and because they are secretive creatures, hiding during the day and hunting at night, you are not likely to see them unless you search patiently.

The bobcat, also called the wildcat, is a relative of the lynxes and resembles the Canada lynx, but is smaller and lighter. It is usually about three feet long at maturity and may weigh as much as forty pounds, though the normal weight is between fifteen and twenty-five pounds. Its coat is pale tan above, spotted with black, and nearly white beneath; its ears are slightly tufted; its tail is very short, which accounts for its name. The hind legs are longer than the forelegs, which gives the animal an awkward, bounding gait when it runs.

If you see a bobcat before it sees you, it will probably be during the day when the animal is sleeping under a thicket or on a ledge, digesting the meal it has caught the night before. Or you may glimpse one walking in the distance at twilight. As soon as the cat becomes aware of you, it will leap away. If you chase it, you may force it to climb a tree or dodge into a hole, since the bobcat is notably short-winded; but you won't have much chance of running it down. It is an agile, clever, sure-footed animal, and a good swimmer as well, so it will do you no good to force it into the water.

It is a ferocious animal, too. Not that it will attack you; tales of bobcats dropping on people from trees make good stories, but none has been authenticated. Yet a bobcat in a trap can be almost unbelievably ferocious, and people who have taken bobcat kittens for pets have often regretted it: they can become vicious on a moment's notice. Moreover, bobcats have no use for their domestic cousins or for dogs; they often attack pet cats and dogs on sight.

They kill poultry too and, if hungry enough, sometimes attack lambs. This gives them a bad reputation, but the bobcat's normal diet consists of rabbits, rats, and other small animals, and its usefulness as a control on these species far outweighs the damage it does. The number of rabbits killed by the average bobcat in its lifetime would be enough to destroy whole crops of vegetables.

A bobcat kitten is relatively tame but becomes dangerous as it matures. The kittens are born in litters of one to four and weigh about eight to twelve pounds by the first fall. Both parents help rear the young cats.

186

In southern sandy deserts a light-colored subspecies called Bailey's bobcat predominates—another case of an animal with a coat that blends with its surroundings. But this is only part of the bobcat's versatility. Its normal range includes many types of habitat—forests, deserts, mountains, plains. The tough and wily bobcat survives in them all.

The same is true of the mountain lion. Various subspecies of this splendid animal occur from Canada to the southern tip of South America, although now in greatly diminished numbers. In many forests of the eastern United States, as in New England and Pennsylvania, mountain lions have been almost if not wholly exterminated, chiefly by hunters who sought the bounties that were offered until recently for dead animals.

Stockier than the jaguar, smaller and less beautifully marked, the mountain lion nevertheless is a magnificent wild beast, often nine feet long and weighing as much as two hundred pounds. Frequently it is pictured by artists silhouetted against the moon, crouched on a tree limb and waiting to spring down on an unwary deer. It makes a picturesque, somewhat eerie scene; and as a matter of fact it does portray the lion's favorite method of hunting. But in open desert country, where there are no big trees, mountain lions hunt their prey by stalking.

Called also cougar, puma, and panther, the mountain lion

A cat of open brushy country, the bobcat hunts for hares, rabbits, small rodents, and occasional birds. A full meal equals about three-fifths of a pound of meat.

is colored a nearly uniform reddish or brownish in summer and a grayish in winter, somewhat darker near the head and at the tip of the tail. In northern forests the coat is normally thick and heavy. In the desert it is lighter and thinner.

Like bobcats, mountain lions trouble farmers and ranchers by attacking unwary domestic animals, and in extremely rare cases they have been known to attack men. These are the reasons for the bounties that have been paid in most states for dead mountain lions. But it would be a serious mistake to eliminate the mountain lion altogether, and in fact its numbers ought to be increased. Mountain lions are an effective check on the population of deer and rodents, which can multiply rapidly and create an even worse problem for farmers.

The great circle

Turning southward again you enter the Mojave Desert, located chiefly in southern Nevada and southern California. You are back in the sandy desert of cactus and creosote bush.

But the outstanding plant of the Mojave Desert is the yucca, especially the species called Joshua tree, a strange plant that branches grotesquely and is protected with sharp-pointed leaves. Its curious shape gives it an unworldly appearance. It may grow to a height of forty feet, and in some places grows in dense forests. When there is enough rainfall, the Joshua tree blossoms once a year, producing lilylike flowers that attract many moths and other insects, although the animal most closely associated with the Joshua tree is the yucca night lizard.

This is one of the smallest desert lizards, no more than three inches long, including its slender tail. It lives among fallen Joshua trees, hiding in the crevices of the dead, scale-like leaves, where it also finds the insects it eats. If you want

The yucca night lizard changes color from clove brown in the daytime to light cream at night. If frightened after nightfall, it becomes darker in color in about a minute.

Because of its attacks on domestic animals, the mountain lion has been so systematically hunted down by man that it is now rare. This great cat, weighing as much as 200 pounds, is extremely agile. It can jump upward a distance of fifteen feet and spring downward sixty feet.

to find a night lizard, pick up a dead Joshua tree branch and shake it. The lizard will very likely fall out and scamper away.

Like many other lizards, the night lizard can change color; this ability probably serves as a protective device. Its basic color is gray or olive, but it is darker during the day than at night—and in spite of its name it seems to be active during both periods. Sometimes its color will change quite suddenly if it becomes frightened or upset. Moreover, the night lizard shares the typical defense of other lizards: it can part with its tail and grow a new one without suffering any permanent harm. This is a handy escape mechanism when the lizard's tail has been grabbed by an enemy. When the tail is only partly broken, a new one may grow in partnership with the old, giving the lizard a forked tail.

The night lizard's diet is entirely invertebrate—ants, spiders, beetles, termites, ticks, caterpillars. Since it may live as long as three or four years, the number of insects consumed may be enormous. Reptiles, amphibians, and some species of birds are among nature's principal means of controlling the growth of insect populations, which otherwise might get out of hand in a very short time. This is precisely what has happened in some areas where the numbers of lizards, frogs, toads, snakes, and flycatching birds have been diminished through the drainage or pollution of their water sources and the destruction of their burrows. Sometimes the same thing happens when foreign species of insects are introduced in a particular area—the local insect-eaters may not be able to catch them, or may not feed on them at all.

Although the Mojave Desert includes Death Valley, well below sea level, most of it is high country, and the Sierras on the western side rise far into the alpine zone. The landscapes are spectacular along the whole mountain range. Southward you pass into the lower deserts of southern California. This leads you back again into the Sonoran Desert of Arizona, where your desert journey began.

Your desert journey has been a great circle passing through many deserts—Chihuahuan, Painted, Great Basin, Mojave, Sonoran. All these deserts can be subdivided into smaller regions based on topography, climate, and many other factors. Taken all in all, your desert journey has encircled about one-fifth of the entire land surface of the United States.

In any desert region plants grow only in those places where elevation, soil texture, salt content, availability of water, and other factors are right for them. The zonation of a range of hills in the relatively moist desert of Arizona might be broken into these six dimensions:

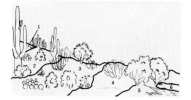

1 Yuccas, agaves, and sotols grow at the highest elevations on eroding mountain slopes where the soil has good drainage and is shallow and rocky.
2 Paloverde, saguaros, and other cactuses such as chollas and prickly pears grow farther down mountain slopes in a zone called the upper bajada.
3 Creosote bush, bur sage, and catclaw are among the plants growing in the finely textured, sandy soil of the lower bajada.
4 Mesquite, lyciums, and jujubes grow in bottom lands where subsurface water is available and the soil has a low salt content.
5 Willows, cottonwoods, and batamote thrive along the edges of stream channels and dry washes that dissect the bottom land.
6 Saltbush, greasewood, and pickleweed are plants that can withstand the highly salty soil of playas and also periodic flooding when rain forms playa lakes.

ORGAN PIPE CACTUS NATIONAL MONUMENT

In southwestern Arizona, on the Mexican border, 516 square miles of the Sonoran Desert were set aside in 1937 for the National Park Service to protect forever a part of the original desert community. Here, on the desert floor or on the slopes of five rugged mountain ranges that reach 5000 feet in height, you can see some of the most spectacular of all desert scenery. Paloverde, smoke trees, mesquite, cat-claws, crucifix thorns, and ocotillo grow in the monument, as well as organ-pipe cactuses, saguaros, night-blooming cereus, and other cactuses. Mammals and birds, such as pronghorns, desert bighorns, peccaries, Gambel's quail, cactus wrens, and road runners, are part of the flourishing animal population.

The organ-pipe cactus, for which the monument is named, grows best on rocky southern slopes. Its many ribbed branches grow upward from ground level and may reach a height of twenty-five feet.

The desert tortoise feeds on wild flowers and other plants until the hottest part of the summer. Then it retreats into its burrow and lives on the fat stored in its body.

The two-foot-long Gila monster is the largest North American lizard. Most lizards feed on insects, but Gila monsters also eat bird and lizard eggs, young birds, and small rodents.

The last frontiers

Great changes are taking place in the desert today. The air that has been pure and clean for millions of years is being polluted with man-made haze and smog. It is still too soon to tell what effect this may have on the desert. We know that smog kills many plants by interfering with respiration and transpiration by clogging breathing pores. Cactuses, which do not have the advantage of renewing foliage periodically, may suffer severely.

But one thing is certain. Nature changes slowly, but man causes rapid changes in the environment. If the pollution of the air continues at its present rate, perhaps the processes of evolution will not keep pace. Fortunately, since man created the pollution of the air, he can also "uncreate" it; he can introduce measures to control the discharge of poisonous wastes into the atmosphere. More and more we are becoming aware of the dangers that arise from the abuse of our natural resources, including the two most precious of all—the air we breathe and the water we drink.

But the desert will change, with or without man's help or hindrance. If you could look into the future, you would see that in a hundred years the desert would be slightly different, in a thousand it would be noticeably altered, and in a hundred thousand it might be almost unrecognizable. But even these spans of time are no more than moments when measured against the millions of years during which the desert has become what it is today.

Millions of people nowadays are finding the desert beautiful, fertile, stimulating, and pleasant beyond their expectations. For this reason more and more desert valleys are being filled with the homes of men. Where long ago Indian huts made of saguaro and ocotillo stood, now subdivisions stretch for miles—thousands of homes made of brick, aluminum, and glass. Where once the Indians cultivated their small patches of corn and squash, now acre after acre of lettuce and broccoli and grove after grove of orange trees grow.

A Navajo Indian tends his meager patch of corn and squash in Monument Valley, Arizona. Corn, squash, and beans have been the major crops of the pueblo-dwelling southwestern Indians for many centuries. The sheep-raising Navajo, a relative latecomer in the area, has adopted the agricultural ways of these ancient people on a smaller scale.

194

Today, vast tracts of desertland are being reclaimed to help support a growing population. Where once only cactuses and mesquite grew, now desert cities stretch out beyond the horizon. Rivers have been heavily tapped, and millions of gallons of water have been pumped from deep within the earth to turn the arid land into fields of lettuce, broccoli, dates, cotton, and other plants.

The problem in the desert now, as it has always been, is water. Although modern man has been able to turn the desert into a fertile and productive land for the time being, water supplies in many areas have been so seriously reduced that strict water-conservation measures must be initiated if the land is not to become arid again.

The desert is rapidly being modified. And in many regions this means it is disappearing, the cold deserts as well as the hot, the badlands of the north and the painted deserts of the south.

In a few reserves and sanctuaries the original desert and its wonderful inhabitants are being kept undisturbed for all time. These are the lands that Stewart Udall, Secretary of the Interior, has called our "special national treasures." There, for all to see, nature enacts her timeless dramas of life and death, drought and flood, regeneration and decay— dramas with heavy meaning for us all.

National parks and wildlife refuges, and state parks and wilderness areas, are the last frontiers. For the most part, communities of plants and animals exist there without disturbance, with no superhighways or subdivisions to edge them out. When you visit these natural sanctuaries, you may find that the desert holds excitement and surprise for you. In your camping, hiking, observing, photographing, studying, you will discover the desert to be a land of unfading fascination—the priceless heritage of the living world of nature.

Scratched out on the sun-baked rocks of a Nevada cliff, the petroglyphs of an ancient Indian artisan are a reminder of the priceless heritage entrusted to us. We are not the first nor will we be the last to marvel at the endless fascinations of the sometimes harsh, always beautiful world of the desert.

199

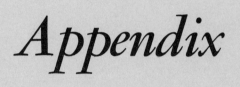

Appendix

National Parks and Monuments in the Southwest

Scattered across the United States is a vast system of national parks, monuments, and recreation areas. From Maine to Hawaii, from Alaska to the Virgin Islands, these priceless areas of wilderness have been set aside by the American people for all to enjoy. Whether desert or plain, forest-covered mountain or wave-washed seashore, each is a superbly scenic area, of matchless scientific value. Each preserves a glimpse into the past, standing as a reminder of what our land looked like before the advent of modern civilization.

The scenic Southwest is particularly rich in national parks and monuments. Many of them are situated in the desert regions described in this book, and others present a striking contrast between desert vegetation at lower elevations and forest vegetation on mountain slopes. The vacationing American who yearns for relief from crowded city pavements can camp at Big Bend or refresh his spirit by gazing at the incomparable panorama of the Grand Canyon. He can swim and sail on Lake Mead or join a guided tour of prehistoric Indian dwellings in Canyon de Chelly. He can drive through the giant cactus forest at Saguaro National Monument, ride horseback along the trails at Zion, stroll across gypsum dunes at White Sands. He can photograph birds and wild flowers. He can find out exactly what a horned lizard looks like and how it lives. Or he might choose to visit an interpretive exhibit and attend an evening talk by a professional naturalist. Whatever his choice of activity, the desert-bound vacationer will find his opportunity in the unique parks and monuments of the American Southwest. Outstanding features of major parks and monuments in the area are described here.

Arches National Monument (Utah)

A fantastic wonderland of eroded rocks. Narrow upright slabs of red sandstone have been carved by water, frost, and wind-blown sand into an incredible maze of windows, pinnacles, spires, and eighty-eight known natural stone arches. Landscape Arch, 291 feet long, is thought to be the longest natural stone span in the world. Ground cover in this high and dry area of the Great Basin Desert includes scattered growths of piñons, junipers, yuccas, and cactuses; wild flowers usually are plentiful in May and June.

DELICATE ARCH

Big Bend National Park (Texas)

A ruggedly beautiful landscape, part desert, part mountain, in the area enclosed by the great bend of the Rio Grande. The park includes three 1500-foot-deep canyons along parts of the river. Of more than 1000 kinds of plants that have been identified within the park, large stands of giant daggers and other yuccas are especially notable. Agave, mesquite, creosote bush, strawberry cactus, and many other plants grow in the area, and there are mixed conifer forests on the cooler heights of the Chisos Mountains. Resident deer herds, peccaries, pronghorns, kit foxes, ringtails, and over 200 kinds of birds give a hint of the abundance of wildlife.

RINGTAIL

Canyon de Chelly National Monument (Arizona)

Spectacular sheer-walled canyon country, including ruins of several hundred prehistoric Indian dwellings that date from 350 to 1200 A.D. Built mostly by Pueblo Indians, some of the ruins are nestled at the bases of the reddish sandstone cliffs, while others perch in caves on the 1000-foot-high canyon walls. White House, Antelope House, and Mummy Cave Ruin are the best known. Modern Navajo Indians still raise vegetables and tend sheep in these beautiful canyons. A few of the animals that live here are prairie dogs, badgers, and porcupines.

Capitol Reef National Monument (Utah)

A twenty-mile-long uplift of colorful sandstone cliffs that rise abruptly from rugged desert country. Wind and water have eroded the rocks into a series of fantastic towers, domes, pinnacles, and gorges. The area is named for the tremendous white dome-shaped formations along the Fremont River. Piñons and junipers predominate, but sagebrush, saltbush, and squawbush also are abundant in this high country near the southeastern margin of the Great Basin Desert.

Carlsbad Caverns National Park (New Mexico)

World renowned for its magnificent underground chambers filled with beautiful mineral deposits, though the surface area of about seventy-five square miles of Chihuahuan desert and semidesert vegetation also is noteworthy. Mesquite and creosote bush are common, as well as claret-cup, barrel, hedgehog, and prickly-pear cactuses. Visit the labeled cactus garden and self-guiding nature trail near the visitor center and watch for collared lizards, race runners, earless lizards, pronghorns, mule deer, and a variety of other wildlife. Another attraction in summer months is the nightly flight of millions of bats from the cave entrance.

Chaco Canyon National Monument (New Mexico)

An archeological monument preserving thirteen superb Indian ruins that represent the highest point in prehistoric Pueblo civilization, as well as hundreds of smaller ruins. Among the largest is Pueblo Bonito, an expertly built "apartment house" of about 800 rooms that spreads over three acres of ground and once rose five stories high. Situated in high plateau country, the monument's vegetation varies from juniper on higher mesas to saltbush and greasewood on the canyon floor. Scaled quail, golden eagles, prairie dogs, ground squirrels, jack rabbits, and lizards are common.

Chiricahua National Monument (Arizona)

A scenic reserve of ridge and canyon country in the Chiricahua Mountains of southeastern Arizona. The main attraction is a vast display of weirdly eroded pillarlike rock formations. Although average annual precipitation is about eighteen inches, most of the rain falls in July and August. As a result, canyon bottoms and cool north slopes are densely covered with a variety of trees and other plants, but south-facing slopes exposed to the full heat of the sun are true deserts dotted with yuccas, agaves, and cactuses. Arizona white-tailed deer, coatis, peccaries, and varied bird life are among the animal attractions.

Death Valley National Monument (California, Nevada)

A vast desert solitude hemmed in by jagged mountain ranges. The lowest point in the Western Hemisphere, 282 feet below sea level, is found here. Nearly 550 square miles of the valley floor lie below sea level, while nearby Telescope Peak rises abruptly for 11,331 feet. The area is a fabulous geological showcase, with sand dunes, salt flats, borax deposits, volcanic craters, and examples of wind and water erosion. Except on salt flats, life is abundant and varied; over 600 kinds of plants, 230 species of birds, and a dozen kinds of lizards have been observed here. The valley itself is forbiddingly hot in summer, but the mild climate from October to May lures thousands of visitors to this dramatic landscape.

COATI

Grand Canyon National Park (Arizona)

World-famous for the awesome mile-deep canyon carved by the Colorado River and the fascinating geological history recorded in its rocks. Elevations range from 2000 feet above sea level at the canyon floor to 9000 feet on parts of the North Rim. Climate thus ranges from desert conditions at the bottom of the canyon, with yuccas, cactuses, agaves, and reptiles such as chuckwallas

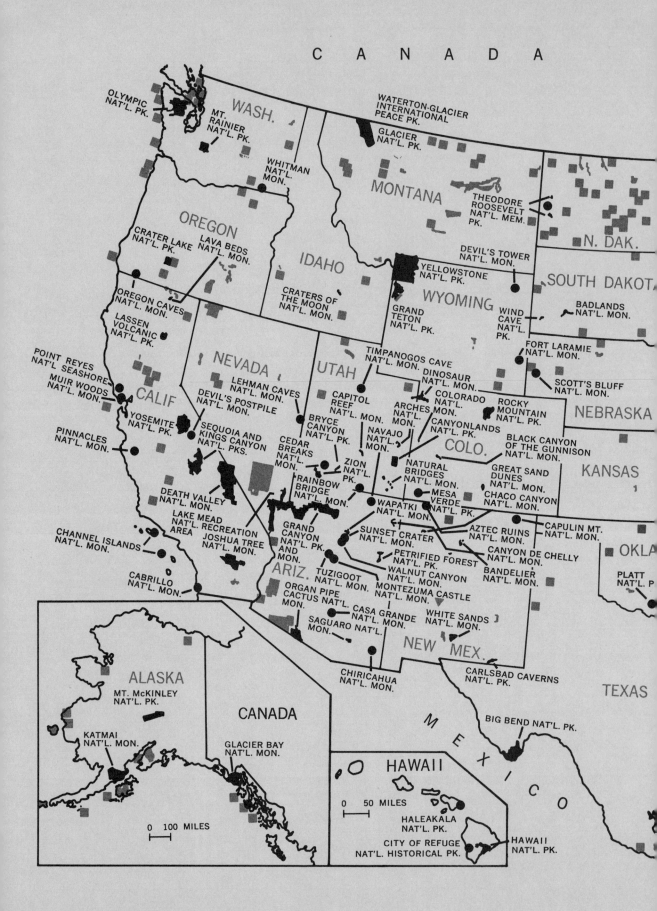

NATIONAL PARKS, MONUMENTS, AND
WILDLIFE REFUGES OF THE UNITED STATES

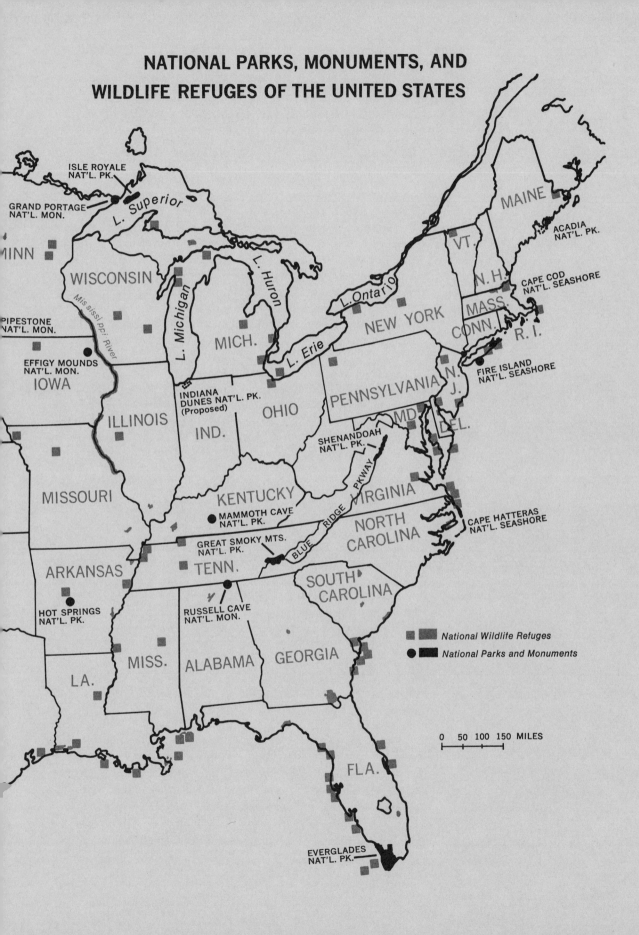

ISLE ROYALE NAT'L. PK.

GRAND PORTAGE NAT'L. MON.

L. Superior

MAINE

ACADIA NAT'L. PK.

MINN

VT.

N. H.

CAPE COD NAT'L. SEASHORE

WISCONSIN

L. Huron

MASS.

NEW YORK

CONN.

R. I.

PIPESTONE NAT'L. MON.

Mississippi River

MICH.

L. Michigan

L. Ontario

L. Erie

PENNSYLVANIA

N. J.

FIRE ISLAND NAT'L. SEASHORE

EFFIGY MOUNDS NAT'L. MON.

IOWA

ILLINOIS

IND.

INDIANA DUNES NAT'L. PK. (Proposed)

OHIO

MD.

DEL.

SHENANDOAH NAT'L. PK.

KENTUCKY

MAMMOTH CAVE NAT'L. PK.

VIRGINIA

RIDGE PKWAY

BLUE

NORTH CAROLINA

CAPE HATTERAS NAT'L. SEASHORE

MISSOURI

GREAT SMOKY MTS. NAT'L. PK.

ARKANSAS

TENN.

SOUTH CAROLINA

HOT SPRINGS NAT'L. PK.

RUSSELL CAVE NAT'L. MON.

National Wildlife Refuges

National Parks and Monuments

MISS.

ALABAMA

GEORGIA

LA.

0 50 100 150 MILES

FLA.

EVERGLADES NAT'L. PK.

and pink rattlesnakes, to cool Canadian conditions on the North Rim, where the forests of spruce, fir, and aspen are especially beautiful. Prehistoric Indian dwellings are situated in canyon walls and on adjacent plateaus, and modern Havasupai, Navajo, and Hopi Indians still live in the area.

Great Sand Dunes National Monument (Colorado)
The largest sand dunes in the United States, stretching out over 57 square miles in a mountain park surrounded by the 14,000-feet-high peaks of the Sangre de Cristo Mountains. Many of these dunes are nearly 1000 feet high. The valley floor surrounding the sandy expanse is covered with sagebrush dotted with aspens, cottonwoods, junipers, and ponderosa and piñon pines. A large spring at the southwestern edge of the sand dunes, thought to be the re-emergence of a river that skirts the dunes for several miles and then disappears, supports a flourishing population of ducks during migration.

Joshua Tree National Monument (California)
In addition to impressive stands of Joshua trees, this scenic desert preserve harbors an astonishing variety of other plants and animals, including a vast natural garden of cholla cactuses. Desert bighorn sheep live here, as well as kangaroo rats, antelope ground squirrels, badgers, kit foxes, chuckwallas, and side-blotched lizards. Especially noteworthy are several natural oases ringed by native California fan palms and other water-loving plants. The edges of these shaded pools are particularly good places for observing throngs of birds and other wildlife.

SNOWY EGRET

Lake Mead National Recreation Area (Arizona, Nevada)
Central features are Lake Mead and Lake Mojave on the Colorado River. (Hoover Dam at the head of Lake Mead is the highest dam in the Western Hemisphere.) Besides splendid opportunities for water sports, the area boasts one of the largest Joshua tree forests in the Southwest. A few desert bighorn are found in the larger canyons and on the higher slopes, and mountain lions and wild burros are sighted occasionally. Since the lakes are the only sizable bodies of water for many miles around, they provide a haven in the heart of the desert for over sixty species of waterfowl and wading birds.

Organ Pipe Cactus National Monument (Arizona)
Named for its impressive stands of organ-pipe cactus, a species that is rare in the United States. Giant saguaros, the rare senita cactus, night-blooming cereus, and nearly thirty other kinds of cactuses thrive in this beautiful desert on the Mexican border. There are also ocotillo, paloverde, elephant trees, and, in season, a fabulous array of wild flowers. The varied habitats range from

208

creosote-bush flats to windswept mountaintops, each supporting a wealth of wildlife. Particularly interesting residents are the Gila monster, desert tortoise, and desert pupfish.

Petrified Forest National Park (Arizona)

A large park including six separate areas of fossilized tree logs 150 to 160 million years old, in addition to ancient Indian ruins and writings. It is surrounded by the Painted Desert, with severely eroded badlands that are noted for the constantly changing quality of their vivid colors. Despite relatively scant vegetation, pronghorns, jack rabbits, ground squirrels, and many other animals manage to survive in the desert.

Saguaro National Monument (Arizona)

A spectacular forest of towering saguaros in a desert backed by rugged mountain ranges. Cholla, prickly-pear, and barrel cactuses also are abundant, plus mesquite, paloverde, ocotillo, and many others. Watch especially for Gila woodpeckers, gilded flickers, and elf owls, as well as badgers, peccaries, mule deer, and kit foxes. The height of the blooming season for colorful carpets of annual wild flowers comes in April, while the cactuses bloom most profusely in May.

YUCCA

White Sands National Monument (New Mexico)

A large area of pure white gypsum dunes, ten to forty-five feet high. Evaporation of water in nearby Lake Lucerno results in deposits of gypsum grains that are carried northeast to the dunes by prevailing winds. Though largely barren, the shifting dunes support a few plants such as squawbush, yuccas, shrubby pennyroyal, saltbush, and cottonwoods. In a few places there are gypsum pedestals, columns of sand grains bound together by tangled roots where plants once grew atop dunes that have since moved on. Pocket mice and species of insects and lizards living in the monument have evolved into pale forms matching the color of the sand.

Zion National Park (Utah)

Impressive canyon and mesa scenery, with narrow sheer-walled canyons and enormous individual rock formations streaked with red, white, orange, and pink. Desert conditions prevail at lower elevations, supporting a sparse cover of yuccas and cactuses, but luxuriant thickets of trees and shrubs grow near rivers and springs. Coniferous trees predominate at higher elevations. Because of many springs at places such as Hanging Gardens and Weeping Rock, Zion offers an array of water-loving flowers and ferns that is equaled in few places in the arid Southwest. The abundant wildlife in the park includes deer, kit foxes, coyotes, road runners, and a variety of reptiles.

Tracks and Trails

With a little practice, anyone can learn to read animal tracks. Look for them in the powdery soil of dry washes, in mud near water holes, or in sand dunes. By noting their size and shape, the number of toes on each foot, claw marks, tail prints, and the arrangement of the tracks, you will usually be able to identify the animal easily. And by watching for feeding signs, dens, and other clues along the trail, you can piece together many details of the animal's habits. Tracks of several desert creatures are shown here. In the case of four-footed animals, prints of right forefoot (*left*) and hind foot (*right*) are shown. The trails indicate the typical pattern of tracks that the animal leaves when moving at moderate speed.

ROAD RUNNER

KANGAROO RAT

BADGER

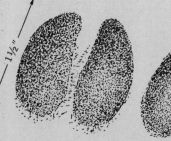

PECCARY

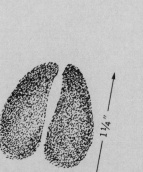

KIT FOX

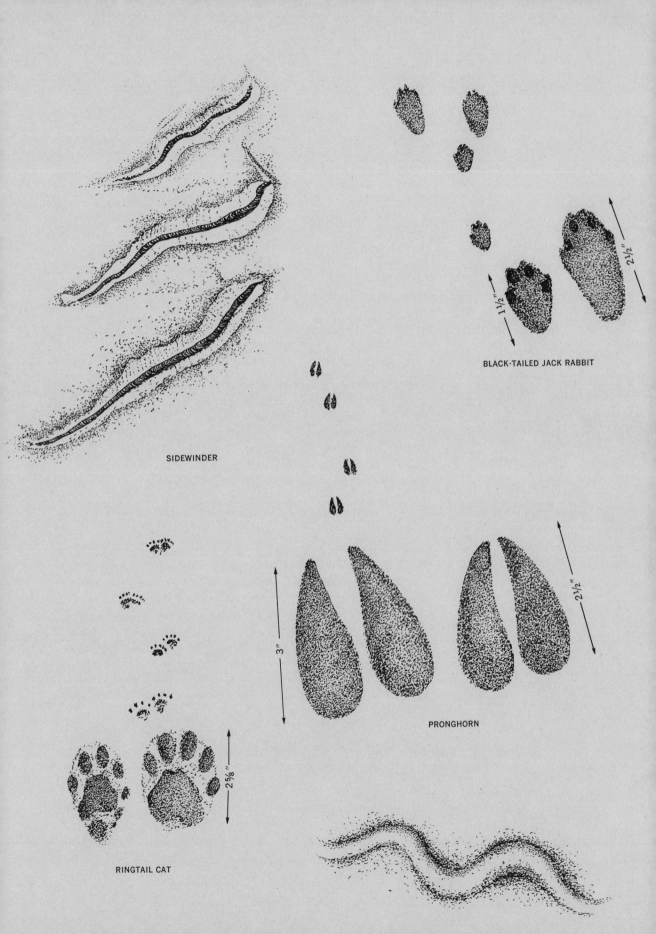

SIDEWINDER

BLACK-TAILED JACK RABBIT

PRONGHORN

RINGTAIL CAT

DIAMONDBACK RATTLESNAKE

Endangered Desert Animals

Few places on earth have intimidated man more than deserts. Their merciless heat, parched air, and seemingly lifeless expanses have discouraged all but the most determined individuals from trespass. In the United States, at least, this has all changed: now it is man himself who threatens the desert and its fragile ecology.

Doubtless, the greatest changes come about when man, through irrigation, transforms arid stretches into vast croplands. To do this, he may obtain water by tapping underground supplies. This, in turn, lowers the water table, thereby decreasing the amount of water available to plants. When the plant life—the basis of any community—is changed, the whole community is drastically altered.

BIGHORN SHEEP

Federal refuges were set aside in Arizona and Nevada just in time to save the desert bighorn from extermination. However, poaching is a serious problem because Congress does not appropriate enough money for adequate warden supervision. At the Desert Game Range, about twenty-five miles north of Las Vegas, on U.S. 95, you can see a small captive herd of this very shy desert sheep.

GILA MONSTER

There are some 3000 species and subspecies of lizards in the world, but only the Gila monster and its Mexican relative are poisonous. Once a common sight in our southwestern deserts, this beautiful slow-moving reptile has been relentlessly persecuted by persons who were certain that they did a good deed whenever they killed one. Now the Gila monster is so rare that in Arizona, at least, it is illegal to molest one. You are not likely to see this unique creature unless you search for it at night.

Grazing on government lands is still a serious threat to desert life. Nowhere is this more dramatically illustrated than in areas inhabited by that unique desert symbol, the saguaro cactus. Grasses and shrubs act as "nurse plants," protecting young saguaros from hungry rodents. Nurse plants that are eaten by cattle are replaced by prickly-pear cactuses. Then the population of rodents that feed on prickly pears increases, and, along with the prickly pears, many small saguaros are eaten.

The day is fast approaching when we shall be able to study and enjoy the life of the desert only in our national parks, refuges, and forests. On these pages are shown some of the desert animals whose existence is particularly threatened.

PUPFISH

President Harry S. Truman issued a Presidential Proclamation adding Devil's Hole, at Ash Meadows, Nevada, to Death Valley National Monument. In doing so, he has helped to preserve one of a very few species of pupfish which live in small salty bodies of water. The spring at Ash Meadows measures only fifteen by forty feet. A larger spring—Quitobaquito—at Organ Pipe Cactus National Monument, Arizona, protects another species. The ever-increasing use of underground water for irrigation presents a very real threat that these springs may become dry, with the result that the remaining few species of this relict population of fish would die.

KIT FOX

This handsome member of the fox tribe is, unfortunately, the least "foxy." Because it is unsuspicious, it is easily trapped and, worse yet, it bolts down poisoned bait intended for coyotes, bobcats, and other predators that man continues to destroy. It would be a great tragedy if we permit this spirit of the desert to be wiped out.

Poisonous Desert Animals

There is nothing particularly frightening about poisonous animals. In fact, animals that possess this remarkable adaptation for subduing prey are among the most interesting of all desert creatures. More important, these venomous creatures are not nearly so dangerous as most people think. In the case of the diamondback rattlesnake, considered one of the most dangerous of all poisonous reptiles, the chances of fatality are less than 2 per cent if proper care is given to a person who is bitten. Then too, there are creatures that are often thought to be poisonous which, in fact, are not. The tarantula is a good example. The stories of its enormous size, its deadly bite, and its prodigious leaps are all false. Scorpions are often regarded as particularly dangerous, but, except for one species, they merely inflict extremely painful stings.

A few simple precautions can reduce the threat of bites and stings by poisonous animals to desert visitors. If you are traveling in back country, wear high-topped leather boots, watch your step, and don't put your hands into holes or crevices. Remember that most snakes, including the poisonous ones, are active after dark, so use a light. Hiking in the desert can be a rewarding experience, but it is only common sense to take along a partner in case of trouble, whether it result from the bite of a poisonous animal or some other mishap. Finally, although it is unlikely that you will be bitten, you should take along a snakebite kit, which can be purchased in any drugstore. As one scientist has very rightly observed, in connection with the Gila monster, anyone who molests it enough to be bitten deserves to be. This is true of other poisonous creatures as well.

Sonoran Coral Snake (*twelve to twenty inches long*)

The slender Sonoran coral snake has a black snout and red rings bordered on each side by yellow ones to the tip of its tail. It lives only in southern Arizona and New Mexico. Secretive and seldom seen, this relative of the cobras probably spends much of its time underground. Its venom undoubtedly is highly dangerous, but there are no known records of humans being bitten.

CORAL SNAKE

Western Diamondback Rattlesnake (*three to six feet long*)
This snake is probably the most dangerous of all the poisonous
creatures in the desert. However, almost every case on record
of a human being bitten by the diamondback can be traced to
carelessness. The poison is injected with two sharp needlelike
fangs that fold back in the snake's mouth. Two little heat-sensitive
pits between the eyes and nostrils on each side of the diamondback's head help it track down the small warm-blooded animals
that make up nearly its entire diet. No rattlesnake is aggressive,
and they often give adequate warning of their presence by the
buzzing sound produced by the rattles at the tip of their tails.

Sidewinder (*eighteen to thirty inches long*)
This small, mostly nocturnal rattlesnake lives in sandy areas of
southwestern Arizona, southern California, and southern Nevada.
It has a distinctive hornlike projection over each eye and moves
by looping sideways in J-shaped curves. Care should be taken
to avoid its bite even though it is less dangerous than that of
most rattlesnakes.

SIDEWINDER

Scorpion (*one to five inches long*)
The scorpion, a near relative of spiders, hunts by night and stings
its prey with a poisonous spine at the tip of its tail. Although
painful, the sting is seldom dangerous to adult humans. One two-
inch-long species from southern Arizona, however, inflicts stings
that may be fatal to children. Since scorpions seek shelter at
dawn, campers should shake out clothing and shoes before putting them on. Otherwise, enjoy its scuttling pursuit of prey and
watch for females carrying broods of newborn young on their
backs.

SCORPION

Gila Monster (*two feet long*)
The rounded black and pinkish scales of the Gila monster resemble Indian beadwork. This lizard hunts after dark for birds' eggs,
insects, and small rodents. Since it is generally slow and sluggish,
the Gila monster, the only poisonous lizard in the United States,
is not likely to bite unless persistently goaded. But when it does
strike, it hangs on tightly and gnaws poison into the wound. If
you are lucky enough to see this rare lizard, don't molest it.

GILA MONSTER

215

Lizards in the Desert

From the tiny yucca night lizard (only three or four inches long) to the two-foot-long Gila monster, the lizards of the Southwest have developed a surprising variety of forms and colors. The most abundant and characteristic of all desert reptiles, they are fascinating, harmless, and relatively easy to observe.

Like all reptiles, lizards are cold-blooded; their body temperatures vary with external temperatures. Although a few give birth to living young, most species lay eggs. All lizards are covered by scales, sometimes fine and granular as on the geckoes, sometimes coarse and overlapping as on spiny lizards. Some of the scales on horned lizards are modified into stout spines.

A few species are legless, but most lizards have four legs, each one tipped by five clawed toes. With the exception of the chuckwalla and the desert crested lizard, which are vegetarians, lizards are active predators whose keen eyes are especially good at detecting movement. Although they have strong teeth, lizards do not chew their food; they simply crush their prey slightly and swallow it whole. Several common species are pictured here. Learn to recognize them, then watch for lizards in your desert travels.

WESTERN BANDED GECKO (four to six inches long) is yellowish with brown spots or crossbands. Hiding by day beneath yucca stems, boards, and other objects, it emerges at dusk to stalk beetles and other small prey. Unlike most lizards, it squeaks noisily when molested.

GREATER EARLESS LIZARD (five to eight inches long) is dull gray, inconspicuous except for the dark bars in front of its hind legs and on the underside of its tail. It differs from most lizards in that it lacks external ear openings. A wary, fast-moving insect-eater, it lives in rocky and brushy areas and often hides under stones.

LEOPARD LIZARD (twelve to fifteen inches long) is grayish with dusky spots and lighter crossbars. It lives throughout the Southwest in gravelly and sandy areas with scattered low bushes. A fast and wary predator, it feeds on all sorts of insects and even eats smaller lizards.

ZEBRA-TAILED LIZARD (six to nine inches long) is pale gray and speckled, with two rows of dark spots down its back. The males have two distinct bars behind their forelegs. When the lizard darts away with its tail curled up, stripes across its underside are especially conspicuous. This speedy predator often catches insects on the run.

COLLARED LIZARD (twelve to fourteen inches long) is brown, gray, olive, even bright green, with light flecks and crossbars and an unmistakable double collar. Found on rocky slopes throughout the Southwest, it leaps nimbly from boulder to boulder and often runs on its hind legs. This voracious predator usually attempts to bite when handled.

SAND LIZARD (six to nine inches long) is white or buff with black markings. Almost invisible against fine wind-blown sand, it lives on dunes in southern California and extreme southwestern Arizona. Fringed toes help this insect-eater run across the sand and bury itself with lightning speed.

DESERT SPINY LIZARD (eight to ten inches long) is dull yellowish or brownish, with rough shingled scales. Widespread in rocky and brushy areas, it eats insects and occasionally other lizards. It usually remains on the ground but can easily climb tree trunks, rocks, and even the sides of buildings.

LONG-TAILED BRUSH LIZARD (five to seven inches long) is dull gray with darker crossbands and has a strip of enlarged scales down the center of its back. Found in southern California and western Arizona, this insect-eater often conceals itself by changing color and stretching out on branches of creosote bush and other shrubs.

SIDE-BLOTCHED LIZARD (four to six inches long) is dull and speckled, with a dark patch behind each foreleg. Common throughout the Southwest, it is the most abundant species in many areas. In southern deserts this insect-eater often remains active throughout the winter.

WESTERN WHIPTAIL (nine to twelve inches long) is long-tailed and slender; dark spots form vague lines down its back. The scales on its back are fine and granular; those on its tail are large and keeled, and form distinct rings. Fond of insects, spiders, and scorpions, it seems to thrive everywhere in the Southwest.

218

Experiments with Desert Soil

Does desert soil act like blotting paper?

In order to test the ability of various types of soil to absorb water, first cut both ends from an empty tin can to form a cylinder. Press the can one inch deep into soil and fill it with water; then measure the time required for the water to soak into the soil. Repeat the test in several types of soil, such as sod on a lawn, spongy soil on the forest floor, and bare hard-packed soil on a path.

Which soil soaks up water fastest? Which is least able to absorb moisture? Dig up a sample of each type of soil to see whether it contains worms or insects. Did they affect the results of the experiment? Does the amount of humus in the soil affect the results? If rain cannot soak readily into soil, what happens to the water during a storm? Does the hard-packed nature of desert soil help to explain the occurrence of flash floods?

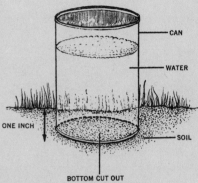

Does a downpour make a difference?

To compare the effects of a downpour and of a gentle rain on soil's ability to absorb water, fill a shallow box (about twelve by twenty inches) with soil. Put a board under one end of the box to form a moderate slope so that water cannot puddle on the surface. Create a gentle shower by shaking water from a laundry sprinkler over the top of the slope. Does most of the water run off, or does some seep into the soil? Dig in the box to see how deeply the water has penetrated.

Now fill the box with fresh soil and repeat the test. Pour the same amount of water from the same height, but this time use a watering can so that the water falls in a steady stream. What happens during the downpour? Does the water penetrate the soil, or does most of it run off? Which is more valuable to desert plants—a cloudburst or a gentle rain? Which is more likely to result in a flash flood?

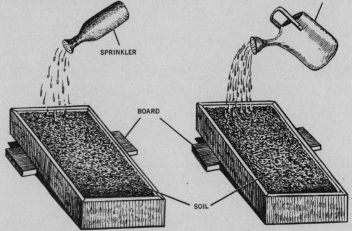

Do soils differ in their ability to store water?

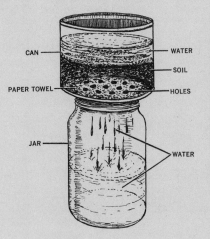

Collect several tin cans, all of the same size. Using a heavy nail and a hammer, punch drainage holes in the bottom of each, from the inside out. Then line the bottom of each can with a circle of paper towel. Pack the cans half full with soil, using a different type in each. Use pure sand in one; a mixture of sand, clay, and humus in another; pure humus; sand and humus; and so on. Place each can over the mouth of a jar, and then pour an equal amount of water (two cups or so) over the soil in each. Does water drain more rapidly through some of the soils than through others? When water stops dripping from the cans, are all the jars equally full? If not, what happened to the water? Squeeze the pure humus to find out.

In the desert most of the dead leaves and other organic matter are blown away or carried off by floods instead of being mixed with the soil. Does this affect the ability of desert soil to store rain water that falls on it? Does this test also help to explain the scarcity of plants on sand dunes?

What about wind? Does moving air cause erosion?

Fill a shallow box with fine dry sand. Cut a cardboard carton to form a shield and place it at one end of the box. Place an electric fan at the opposite end of the box and let it run for several minutes. Measure the amount of sand blown against the shield. Replace the sand in the box, but this time poke tufts of weeds or evergreen boughs into the surface of the sand. Run the fan for the same length of time and again measure the amount of sand removed by the breeze. Explain the difference. Does scarcity of vegetation on the desert increase the danger of wind erosion?

If you live in a cold climate, you can observe large-scale wind erosion in winter. The material moved by the wind is snow instead of soil, but the results are similar. Does the snow keep moving indefinitely, or is it deposited in drifts? Do slopes, hedges, and trees affect the formation of snow drifts? Might similar surface features affect formation of sand dunes?

Does evaporation rate affect the desert's water supply?

Soak several paper towels in water, and place them on the ground in different areas to see whether all dry out at the same rate. (Weight the corners with stones to prevent the towels from blowing away as they dry.) Place one towel where it is exposed to both sun and wind. Put another in full sun where a building or some other obstruction protects it from breezes. Place two more towels in the shade, one exposed to breezes, the other protected from wind. Which towel dries out first? Which remains damp longest? Do sun and wind affect the rate at which water evaporates? Where is soil more exposed to sun and wind—in the desert or in the forest? Dig up some soil from each area tested. Does it seem moister in some areas than in others?

Does erosion help shape the landscape?

Use a shallow box as in the second experiment. Fill it with soil, leaving the surface bare on one half and covered with sod on the other. Prop the box slightly to form a gentle slope. First sprinkle water at the head of the grass-covered slope, and then from the same height sprinkle the same amount of water on the bare soil. Do plants help to bind the soil in place? Where is erosion likely to be worse—in a desert or in a forest? Refill the box and repeat the experiment with a steeper slope. Does this affect the rate of erosion?

You can observe water erosion on a larger scale by examining slopes and terraces on lawns and along roads. Which show greater erosion after storms—slopes covered with grass, or new ones where grass is not yet established? Have alluvial fans formed at the bases of some of the gullies on bare slopes?

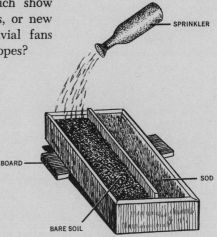

SPRINKLER

BOARD

SOD

BARE SOIL

Glossary

Adaptation: An inherited characteristic that improves an organism's chances for survival in a particular *habitat*. Adaptations may involve the structure (form) or functioning (physiology) of an organism's body, as well as inherited behavioral patterns. In the case of humans, scientists sometimes refer to cultural adaptations, which are learned rather than inherited characteristics of their modes of living that improve their chances for survival.

Alkaline water: Water containing large amounts of dissolved mineral salts.

Alluvial fan: A fan-shaped deposit of rocks, gravel, and sediments that forms where the speed of water in a stream or other channel slows down abruptly, as at the foot of a steep mountain slope.

Alpine zone: The portion of a mountain that lies above *tree line*. *See* Vegetation zones.

Amphibians: The group of animals that includes frogs, toads, and salamanders. Amphibians have soft, moist skins and are characterized by life cycles in which the *larvae* live in water and breathe through gills, while adults live on land and breathe through lungs but return to water to lay their eggs.

Annual: A plant that completes its life cycle from seedling to mature seed-bearing plant during a single growing season, then dies.

Archeology: The scientific study of prehistoric cultures by examination and analysis of their remains. A scientist who specializes in this study is an archeologist.

Arid: Dry; lacking in moisture.

Arroyo: A stream bed or channel in an arid region. Dry most of the time, it carries water only after heavy rainfalls, then quickly dries up again. Also known as a dry wash.

Artesian well: A well in which the nature and configuration of underground rock layers cause water to rise to the surface as a result of natural subterranean pressure.

Association: A grouping of plants or animals that characteristically occur together.

Badlands: An area where soft rocks or clays have been severely eroded and gullied, often into fantastic forms, so that they resemble miniature mountain ranges.

Behavioral adaptation: *See* Adaptation.

Bird display: An instinctive behavior pattern, often involving elaborate posturing, strutting, and other ritualized actions, by which a bird communicates with others of the same *species*; usually associated with activities such as courtship of a mate, territorial defense, or changeover of incubating chores.

Botany: The scientific study of plants. A biologist specializing in this study is a botanist.

Bottom land: Low-lying land along a river course, consisting of sediments deposited by the river in times of flooding.

Bounty: A reward paid by a governmental agency for killing an animal considered harmful to human interests.

Browse: To feed on the twigs and leaves of woody plants. Deer and their relatives are browsers.

Butte: A somewhat narrow columnar erosional remnant rising abruptly from the surrounding landscape. A cap of hard rock usually has slowed down erosion so that the butte remains standing even after surrounding rocks have eroded away. *See* Mesa.

Canyon: A deep, steep-sided valley eroded into the land by the running water of a stream or river.

Chain of life: The interdependence of all forms of life on each other and the ultimate dependence of all life on the energy of the sun; the constant transfer of solar energy from one form of life to another along *food chains.*

Chaparral: Dense scrub vegetation, such as low evergreen oaks.

Chlorophyll: A group of pigments that produces the green color of plants; essential to *photosynthesis.*

Climate: The average weather conditions of an area, including temperature, rainfall, humidity, wind, and hours of sunlight, based on records kept for many years.

Cold-blooded: Lacking the ability to regulate body temperature, with the result that body temperature fluctuates substantially with variations in external temperature. Because of this the temperature of a cold-blooded animal, such as an insect or *reptile*, may actually be quite warm in warm weather, but in cold weather the animal becomes sluggish or dormant as its temperature falls. *See* Warm-blooded.

Cold desert: A *desert* of middle or northern latitudes or high elevations, where daytime temperatures are moderate or low through much of the year. As a result, rainfall usually is higher than in *hot deserts*, and moisture evaporates more slowly. The characteristic dominant plant of the Great Basin Desert, the most extensive cold desert in North America, is sagebrush.

Community: All the plants and animals that live in a particular *habitat* and are bound together by *food chains* and other interrelations.

Competition: The struggle between individuals or groups of living things for common necessities, such as water or living space.

Compost: A mixture of the decaying remains of dead plants and animals.

Conservation: The use of natural resources in a way that assures their continuing availability to future generations; the wise use of natural resources.

Cultural adaptation: *See* Adaptation.

Cumulonimbus cloud: A billowing mountainlike cloud mass characteristic of thunderstorm conditions.

Desert: A region where average annual rainfall is less than ten inches and the rain is unevenly distributed through the year. As a result of these conditions, plant cover is fairly sparse and restricted to plants adapted to survival where water is scarce. *See* Cold desert; Hot desert.

Drought: A prolonged period when little or no moisture falls on an area.

Dry wash: *See* Arroyo.

Dust bowl: An area where plant cover has been severely damaged by improper farming methods, prolonged drought, or both, permitting wind to blow away the unprotected topsoil.

Ecology: The scientific study of the relationships of living things to one another and to their *environment.* A scientist who studies these relationships is an ecologist.

Entomology: The scientific study of insects. Biologists who specialize in this study are entomologists.

Environment: All the external conditions surrounding a living thing.

Erosion: The wearing away of areas of the earth's surface by water, wind, ice, and other natural forces.

Estivation: A prolonged dormant or sleeplike state that enables an animal to escape the rigors of survival during summer months in a hot climate. As in *hibernation*, body processes such as breathing and heartbeat slow down drastically, and the animal neither eats nor drinks.

Evolution: The process of natural consecutive modification in the inherited makeup of living things; the process by which modern plants and animals have arisen from forms that lived in the past.

Flash flood: A sudden destructive rush of water across the desert floor and down *arroyos* after a rainstorm, resulting from the inability of hard-packed desert soil to absorb rain water as quickly as it falls. Besides occurring suddenly, flash floods usually subside quickly.

Flush: To rouse from hiding. Used especially with reference to game birds.

Food chain: A series of plants and animals linked by their food relationships. Green plants, a plant-eating *rodent*, and a rodent-eating *predator* would form a simple food chain. Any one *species* usually is represented on many food chains. *See* Chain of life.

Form: A small protected place, usually a hollow in the grass, where a rabbit or hare rests.

Geology: The scientific study of the earth and the rocks of which it is formed. A scientist who specializes in this study is a geologist.

Habitat: The immediate surroundings (living place) of a plant or animal; everything necessary to life in a particular location except the life itself.

Hare: A lanky rabbitlike animal whose young are born with their eyes opened, their bodies covered with fur, and the ability to move about soon after birth. The young of rabbits, in contrast, are blind, naked, and helpless at birth.

Hibernation: A prolonged dormant or sleeplike state that enables an animal to escape the difficulties of survival during winter months in a cold climate. *See* Estivation.

Hot desert: A *desert* of subtropical latitudes or low elevations, where daytime temperatures throughout the year are high.

Creosote bush and *succulents* are the characteristic dominant plants of hot deserts in the American Southwest. *See* Cold desert.

Humidity, relative: The ratio of the amount of water vapor actually present in air of a given temperature as compared with the greatest possible amount that could be present in air at that temperature. Usually expressed as a percentage.

Hybrid: Resulting from the interbreeding of individuals of different *species.*

Larva (plural *larvae*): An active immature stage in an animal's life history, during which its form differs from that of the adult, such as the caterpillar stage in the development of a butterfly or the tadpole stage in the life history of a frog.

Mammals: The group of animals including *rodents*, humans, bats, and many other forms. All are *warm-blooded*, possess special milk-producing glands, are at least partially covered by hair, and usually bear their young alive.

Mesa: A somewhat extensive flat-topped landform bounded by steep cliffs that rise abruptly from the surrounding landscape. Capped by a layer of hard rock, it has resisted erosion more effectively than the highlands that once surrounded it. *See* Butte; Plateau.

Metabolic water: Water produced by all animals as a by-product of digestion, resulting from the recombination of hydrogen and oxygen released in the digestion of sugars. Although the amount of water thus produced is small, some animals, such as kangaroo rats and meal worms, are so efficient at conserving it that metabolic water is sufficient to maintain proper balance of their body fluids.

Microhabitat: A miniature *habitat* within a larger one, such as a wet area in the desert. Since environmental conditions differ from those in the surrounding area, the microhabitat supports its own distinctive self-sustaining *community* of plants and animals.

Microorganism: A plant or animal too small to be seen without magnification.

Mirage: An optical illusion in which distant objects appear as reflections on the surface of a layer of heated air.

Niche, ecological: An organism's role in a natural *community*, such as seed-eater, daytime *predator*, or nighttime predator. Refers to the organism's function, not the place where it is found.

Nurse plant: A plant that provides shade for a seedling unable to withstand prolonged exposure to the sun during the early stages of its growth.

Oasis: An area in a desert where a natural or artificial water source supports a *community* of plants that could not survive the arid conditions of the desert itself.

Overgrazing: Excessive feeding on the vegetation of an area by wild or domestic animals; results in serious and often lasting damage to the area's ability to support desirable plant life.

Pediment: A long gentle slope extending out from the foot of a mountain; composed of gravel, sand, and boulders eroded from the mountainside.

Photosynthesis: The process by which green plants convert carbon dioxide and water into simple sugars. *Chlorophyll* and sunlight are essential to the series of complex chemical reactions involved.

Physiological adaptation: *See* Adaptation.

Pigment: A chemical substance that imparts color to an object by reflecting or transmitting only certain light rays.

Plateau: An extensive flatland of high elevations, dissected by many steep valleys and canyons. *See* Mesa.

Playa: A "dry lake"; a natural basin in a desert valley where run-off water collects after rainfalls. Since the basin has no outlet, the water eventually evaporates or seeps into the earth, leaving the lake bed paved with salt deposits.

Pollution: The fouling of a resource such as air or water with gases, industrial wastes, sewage, or other contaminants that make it unfit to support many forms of life.

Potash: A mineral salt (a form of potassium) often found in abundant deposits in deserts or former desert areas.

Prairie: Grassland; an area where the average annual rainfall (usually ten to thirty inches) is more than in a *desert*, but not enough to support the growth of forests.

Predator: An animal that lives by capturing other animals for food. *See* Prey.

Prey: A living animal that is captured for food by another animal. *See* Predator.

Reptiles: The group of animals including snakes, lizards, turtles, alligators, and others. Reptiles typically are covered by scales or horny plates, breathe by means of lungs, lay eggs, and usually live on land.

Rodents: The large group of gnawing *mammals* including rats, mice, squirrels, beavers, and many others. Characterized by possession of a pair of long, chisel-like teeth at the front of both upper and lower jaws, used for gnawing and clipping plant foods.

Saline: Salty.

Saltern: A flat field or pool where sea water is allowed to evaporate in order to extract its salt content.

Salt-tolerant plant: A plant able to grow in soil with a high salt content.

Specialization: The sum of the *adaptations* that enable a plant or animal to survive in a particular *habitat* or equip it for a particular mode of life. Although a highly specialized plant or animal may be well adapted for survival in its own habitat, however, it may be unable to adjust to changes in its habitat or to exploit habitats where living conditions are different.

Species (plural *species*): A group of plants or animals whose members breed naturally only with each other and who resemble each other more closely than they resemble members of any similar group.

Spine: A slender, pointed woody structure on the stem of a cactus; actually a highly modified leaf. A thorn, in contrast, is a modified twig.

Spruce-fir zone: The area on a mountainside just below *tree line* where, because the climate resembles far northern areas, the characteristic tree *association* is a mixture of spruces and firs. *See* Vegetation zones.

Stomate: A microscopic opening in the surface of a leaf that allows gases to pass in and out.

Subspecies (plural *subspecies*): A group of individuals of the same *species* that live within a more or less well-defined geographical area and differ slightly but consistently from individuals of the same species living elsewhere. A single species of plant or animal may include many subspecies.

Succulent: Juicy; containing much moisture. A succulent is a plant, such as cactus or stonecrop (sedum), that stores water in tissues of its stems or leaves during rainy weather and maintains vital functions by drawing on this reserve of moisture in times of drought.

Topography: The sum of the surface features of the land in an area, such as its mountains, canyons, plains, and valleys.

Transpiration: The process by which water evaporates from plant tissues.

Tree line: The upper limit of tree growth on a mountain, usually consisting of a band of stunted and oddly shaped trees. *See* Vegetation zones.

Tuber: A fleshy or thickened underground stem, such as the edible portion of a potato plant.

Vegetation zones: The horizontal belts of distinctive plant cover on mountainsides, resulting from climatic changes related to changes in elevation.

Volcanic plug: A hard core of *lava* that cooled in the throat of a dying volcano and remains standing as a jagged pinnacle after the softer rock, lava, and soil of the surrounding slopes wear away.

Warm-blooded: Able to maintain a fairly constant body temperature in spite of fluctuations in environmental temperature. Of all animals, only birds and *mammals* are warm-blooded. *See* Cold-blooded.

Water hole: Any more or less permanent standing pool of water on desert or rangeland, whether natural or man-made.

Water table: The upper level of the underground reservoir of water, below which the soil and all cracks and channels in the rocks are saturated. The water level in different areas may lie at the surface or hundreds of feet underground and, depending on rainfall and rate of removal of the water, may fluctuate from time to time in any given area.

Wilderness: A tract of land, whether desert, forest, seashore, or any other, where man is only a visitor; an area where the original natural *community* of plants and animals survives in balance and intact, unaltered by mechanized civilization.

Zenith: The point at which the sun appears most nearly directly over an observer's head during the course of a day.

Bibliography

DESERTS

BURNS, WILLIAM A. (Editor). *The Natural History of the Southwest.* Franklin Watts, 1960.

CLOUDSLEY-THOMPSON, J. L., and M. J. CHADWICK. *Life in Deserts.* Dufour Editions, 1964.

GLUECK, NELSON. *Rivers in the Desert.* Farrar, Straus & Cudahy, 1959.

HOWES, PAUL GRISWOLD. *The Giant Cactus Forest and Its World.* Little, Brown, 1954.

JAEGER, EDMUND C. *The North American Deserts.* Stanford University Press, 1957.

KLOTS, ALEXANDER B., and ELSIE B. KLOTS. *The Desert* (Vol. 5, *The Community of Living Things*). Creative Educational Society, 1956.

LEOPOLD, A. STARKER, and THE EDITORS OF LIFE. *The Desert.* Time, Inc., 1961.

POND, ALONZO. *The Desert World.* Nelson, 1962.

SEARS, PAUL B. *Deserts on the March.* University of Oklahoma Press, 1959.

DESERT ANIMALS

BAILEY, VERNON. *Mammals of New Mexico.* U.S. Department of Agriculture, 1931.

BOURLIÈRE, FRANÇOIS. *The Natural History of Mammals.* Knopf, 1964.

DAVIS, WILLIAM B. *The Mammals of Texas.* Texas Game and Fish Commission, 1960.

HALL, E. RAYMOND. *Mammals of Nevada.* University of California Press, 1946.

JAEGER, EDMUND C. *Desert Wildlife.* Stanford University Press, 1961.

LIGON, J. STOKLEY. *New Mexico Birds and Where to Find Them.* University of New Mexico Press, 1961.

LUTZ, FRANK E. *Field Book of Insects.* Putnam, 1948.

MILLER, ALDEN H., and ROBERT C. STEBBINS. *The Lives of Desert Animals in Joshua Tree National Monument.* University of California Press, 1964.

MURIE, OLAUS J. *A Field Guide to Animal Tracks.* Houghton Mifflin, 1954.

OLIN, GEORGE, and J. CANNON. *Mammals of the Southwest Deserts.* Southwestern Monuments Association, 1959.

OLIVER, JAMES A. *The Natural History of North American Amphibians and Reptiles.* Van Nostrand, 1955.

PALMER, RALPH S. *The Mammal Guide.* Doubleday, 1954.

PETERSON, ROGER TORY. *A Field Guide to Western Birds.* Houghton Mifflin, 1961.

PHILLIPS, ALLAN, JOE MARSHALL, and GALE MONSON. *The Birds of Arizona.* University of Arizona Press, 1964.

SCHMIDT, KARL P., and D. DWIGHT DAVIS. *Field Book of Snakes of the United States and Canada.* Putnam, 1941.

SCHMIDT-NIELSEN, KNUT. *Desert Animals: Physiological Problems of Heat and Water.* Oxford University Press, 1964.

SMITH, HOBART M. *Handbook of Lizards.* Comstock, 1946.

STEBBINS, ROBERT C. *Amphibians and Reptiles of Western North America.* McGraw-Hill, 1954.

ZIM, HERBERT S., and HOBART M. SMITH. *Reptiles and Amphibians.* Golden Press, 1956.

DESERT PLANTS

BENSON, LYMAN. *The Cacti of Arizona.* University of Arizona Press, 1950.

BENSON, LYMAN, and ROBERT A. DARROW. *The Trees and Shrubs of the Southwestern Deserts.* University of Arizona Press, University of New Mexico Press, 1954.

BRITTON, N. L., and J. N. ROSE. *The Cactaceae.* Carnegie Institution, 1919–1923.

CARLSON, RAYMOND (Editor). *The Flowering Cactus.* McGraw-Hill, 1954.

DODGE, NATT N. *100 Desert Wildflowers in Natural Color.* Southwestern Monuments Association, 1965.

JAEGER, EDMUND C. *Desert Wild Flowers.* Stanford University Press, 1941.

KEARNEY, THOMAS H., ROBERT H. PEEBLES, and others. *Arizona Flora.* University of California Press, 1960.

PATRAW, PAULINE M., and JEANNE R. JANISH. *Flowers of the Southwest Mesas.* Southwestern Monuments Association, 1964.

SHREVE, FORREST, and IRA L. WIGGINS. *Vegetation and Flora of the Sonoran Desert.* Stanford University Press, 1964.

VINES, ROBERT A. *Trees, Shrubs, and Woody Vines of the Southwest.* University of Texas Press, 1960.

ECOLOGY

ALLEN, DURWARD L. *Our Wildlife Legacy.* Funk & Wagnalls, 1962.

BUCHSBAUM, RALPH, and MILDRED BUCHSBAUM. *Basic Ecology.* Boxwood Press, 1957.

DAUBENMIRE, REXFORD F. *Plants and Environment.* Wiley, 1959.

FARB, PETER, and THE EDITORS OF LIFE. *Ecology.* Time, Inc., 1963.

ODUM, EUGENE P., and HOWARD T. ODUM. *Fundamentals of Ecology.* Saunders, 1959.

SHELFORD, VICTOR E. *The Ecology of North America.* University of Illinois Press, 1963.

GENERAL

BUTCHER, DEVEREUX. *Exploring Our National Parks and Monuments.* Houghton Mifflin, 1960.

HORNADAY, WILLIAM T. *Camp-fires on Desert and Lava.* Scribner, 1908.

KIRK, RUTH. *Exploring Death Valley.* Stanford University Press, 1956.

KRUTCH, JOSEPH WOOD. *The Desert Year.* Sloane, 1952.

KRUTCH, JOSEPH WOOD. *The Voice of the Desert.* Sloane, 1955.

POWELL, JOHN WESLEY. *The Exploration of the Colorado River.* Anchor Books, 1961.

STORER, JOHN H. *The Web of Life.* Devin-Adair, 1960.

TILDEN, FREEMAN. *The National Parks: What They Mean to You and Me.* Knopf, 1951.

UDALL, STEWART L. *The Quiet Crisis.* Holt, Rinehart and Winston, 1963.

Illustration Credits and Acknowledgments

COVER: Red-tailed hawk, Evan J. Davis

UNCAPTIONED PHOTOGRAPHS: 8–9: Prickly-pear and saguaro cactuses in Arizona, Josef Muench 66–67: Thunderstorm in the Sonoran Desert, Manley Photo from Shostal 108–109: Bighorn sheep skull, Death Valley National Monument, California, Peter G. Sanchez 150–151: White Sands National Monument, New Mexico, Peter G. Sanchez

ALL OTHER ILLUSTRATIONS: 10–11: Robert Barbee 12: National Park Service 13: Lewis Wayne Walker 14–15: Felix Cooper 16: Thase Daniel 17: Emil Muench 18: Dale A. Zimmerman 19: Felix Cooper 20: Wilford L. Miller 21–22: Felix Cooper 23: Robert H. Wright 24–25: Myron D. Sutton, National Park Service 26: Mervin W. Larson 27: Monkmeyer 28–29: Lynwood M. Chace 30: Felix Cooper 30–31: William Belknap, Jr. from Rapho-Guillumette 32: Thase Daniel 33: Robert Leatherman 34: Robert Barbee 35: Edward S. Ross 36–37: Richard Jepperson from Photo Researchers 38: Evan J. Davis 39: Dale A. Zimmerman 40–41: Wilford L. Miller 42: Lewis Wayne Walker 43: Peter G. Sanchez 44–45: Charles Fracé 46: Monkmeyer 47: Dale A. Zimmerman 48: Hans Zillessen from G.A.I. 49: Willis Peterson 50: Paul Nesbit; George M. Bradt 51: Dr. Alexander B. Klots; George M. Bradt 52: Bruce Hayward 53: Dr. Alexander B. Klots 54: George M. Bradt 55: Hans Zillessen from G.A.I. 56: Harold J. Brodrick 57: Verna R. Johnston 58–59: Gale Monson 60: Cassidy from Black Star 61: John J. Stophlet 62: Mervin W. Larson 63: Felix Cooper 64: Verna R. Johnston 68: Felix Cooper 69: Josef Muench 70–71: Josef Muench 72: Hans Zillessen from G.A.I. 73: Lawrence R. Owen 74–75: Peter G. Sanchez 76: Willis Peterson; Burkette from Black Star 77: R. Smith from Black Star 78: Graphic Arts International 79: Robert Leatherman 80–81: Robert H. Wright 82–83: Gale Monson 84: Emil Muench; Peter G. Sanchez; Peter G. Sanchez 85: Don Ollis from Black Star; Hiram L. Parent 86: Patricia C. Henrichs 87: Emil Muench 88: Robert Barbee 89: Felix Cooper 90–91: Bob Clemenz 92: Pat Kirkpatrick from Shostal 93: Bob Clemenz 94: Jim Yoakum from Monkmeyer 95: Robert Leatherman 96–97: Hiram L. Parent 98: Hans Zillessen from G.A.I. 99: Peter G. Sanchez 100: Arizona Photographic Associates 101: Ansel Adams 102–103: Charles Fracé 104: Peter G. Sanchez 105: Dale A. Zimmerman 106: Emil Muench 110–111: Bob Clemenz 112: Charles W. Herbert from Western Ways Features 113: Peter G. Sanchez 114: Patricia C. Henrichs 115: Bettmann Archives 116–119: Willis Peterson 120: Dale A. Zimmerman 121–122: Patricia C. Henrichs 123: Peter G. Sanchez 124: National Park Service 125: William A. Niering 126–127: Patricia C. Henrichs 128: Thase Daniel 129: William G. Bass; Harold J. Brodrick; J. M. Conrader 130: Patricia C. Henrichs 131: Hiram L. Parent 132: Dale A. Zimmerman; Robert Leatherman 133: Robert Leatherman from National Audubon Society 134: Lawrence R. Owen; Peter G. Sanchez 135: Josef Muench 136–137: Middleham from Black Star 138: Pat Kirkpatrick from National Audubon Society 139: Robert Leatherman from National Audubon Society 140: Bucky Reeves 141: Willis Peterson 142: Lawrence R. Owen 143: Charles Fracé 144–145: Edward S. Ross 146–147: George M. Bradt 148: Russ Kinne from Photo Researchers 152–153: Graphic Arts International 154–155: Peter G. Sanchez 156: Thase Daniel 157: Willis Peterson 158: Harold J. Brodrick 159: Robert H. Wright from National Audubon Society 160–161: Jack Zehrt from Shostal 162: Arizona Photographic Associates 163: Willis Peterson 164: Ewing Galloway 165–167: Hiram L. Parent 168–169: Lawrence R. Owen 170: William Belknap, Jr. from Rapho-Guillumette 171: Robert Leatherman 172: Roland H. Wauer; Dale A. Zimmerman 173: Dale A. Zimmerman 174: Harry Engels 175: Charles Fracé 176–177: Ewing Galloway 178: David Parmelee 179: Lawrence R. Owen 180–181: Michael Wotton 183–187: Ed Park 188: Wilford L. Miller 189: Robert Leatherman 190–191: Patricia C. Henrichs 192: Arizona Photographic Associates; Verna R. Johnston 193: Ansel Adams 195: Charles W. Herbert from Western Ways Features 196–197: Debs Metzong 198: Shostal 201: Grambs Miller 203–205: Charles Fracé 206–207: Graphic Arts International 208–215: Charles Fracé 216–218: Patricia C. Henrichs 219–221: Charles Fracé

PHOTO EDITOR: ROBERT J. WOODWARD

ACKNOWLEDGMENTS: *The publisher wishes to thank Wayne W. Bryant and William Perry of the National Park Service, both of whom read the entire manuscript and offered valuable suggestions. The editorial assistance of Vincent Manson, Assistant Curator of Mineralogy at the American Museum of Natural History, and Dr. Arthur Cronquist, Senior Curator of the New York Botanical Garden, is also appreciated.*

Index